MANAGING YOUR SELF

Developmental Management

General Editor: Ronnie Lessem

Charting the Corporate Mind
Charles Hampden-Turner*

Managing in the Information Society
Yoneji Masuda

Developmental Management
Ronnie Lessem

Foundations of Business
Ivan Alexander

Ford on Management
Henry Ford*

Managing the Developing Organization
Bernard Lievegoed

Managing Your Self
Jagdish Parikh

Greening Business
John Davis

Conceptual Toolmaking
Jerry Rhodes

* For copyright reasons this edition is not available in the USA

Developmental
MANAGEMENT

Managing Your Self

MANAGEMENT BY DETACHED INVOLVEMENT

JAGDISH PARIKH

With a Foreword by
Juan Rada
and Editor's Introduction
by Ronnie Lessem

BLACKWELL
Business

Copyright © Jagdish Parikh 1991
Foreword © Juan Rada 1991
Editor's Introduction © Ronnie Lessem 1991

First published 1991
Reprinted 1991

Basil Blackwell Ltd
108 Cowley Road, Oxford, OX4 1JF, UK

Basil Blackwell, Inc.
3 Cambridge Center
Cambridge, Massachusetts 02142, USA

British Library Cataloguing in Publication Data
A CIP catalogue record for this book is available from
the British Library.

Library of Congress Cataloging in Publication Data
Parikh, Jagdish.
Managing your self: management by detached involvement / Jagdish
Parikh; with an editor's introduction by Ronnie Lessem.
p. cm.—(Developmental management)
Includes bibliographical references.
ISBN 0–631–17764–7
1. Self-actualization (Psychology) 2. Self-management
(Psychology) 3. Success in business—Psychological aspects.
I. Title. II. Title: Managing yourself. III. Series.
BF637.S4P35 1990
158′.1—dc20 90–33293 CIP

Typeset in 11 on 13 pt Ehrhardt
by Hope Services (Abingdon) Ltd.
Printed in Great Britain by T. J. Press (Padstow) Ltd, Padstow, Cornwall

Contents

CONTENTS

PART III   SELF MANAGEMENT IN SOCIETY

Foreword

There are three main reasons why I believe Dr Jagdish Parikh's book *Managing Your Self* is a significant contribution to the literature for the practicing manager. The first one has to do with the fact that the agenda of business has changed. During the decades just after World War II, the main issue was how to cope efficiently with the pent-up demand in the market, but since the early eighties (or even earlier) the issue has become one of restructuring and revitalizing our corporations. At the beginning of the first time period, analytical skills dominated the profile of the successful manager – we had to be able to select rationally from among many growth options. In contrast, the tasks of today require additional qualities: like imagination, inventiveness, and the capability to understand systems of ever increasing complexity. These qualities – part of a larger shift in our methods of perceiving and capturing reality – build on powers of the personality we have ignored in business for a long time: the power of intuition and management of one's self. Most managers readily admit that decision-making or judgement is a complex mix of analysis, incomplete knowledge and intuition. This shift, with the emphasis being put on intuition, creates a new context in which a good number of managers do not know how to function.

The second reason is that the number of managers who are disenchanted with their work appears to be increasing. They not only fail to get the satisfaction they rightfully should expect from their jobs, but often they find that they are not able to develop their full potential as human beings.

Even managers who, by traditional measures, are unusually successful in their jobs show deficiencies in other areas: while their one-track determination enabled them to become well-paid top achievers, they have great difficulties functioning well in, say, family life and in the community at large. More and more managers seem to yearn for a better equilibrium as human beings, even though it is often difficult to speak about it openly.

Jagdish Parikh's book addresses both clusters of issues. It contributes to answering the question of how to manage the self in order to achieve a healthy balance between the different levels of our existence. In addition, it tries to shed some light on the question of how to reach a high level of performance essential in the context of accelerating change and uncertainty. For this purpose, he introduces the concept of *management by detached involvement* which is a timely contribution to management thinking and practice.

The third distinctive feature of Jagdish Parikh's book is that he has not tried to make an academic book out of this complex subject but rather, he has given a personal testimonial which, having profound value, has also the inevitable limitations of this type of work.

Jagdish Parikh is well equipped to write such a guide to self-management. Although he was born and raised in Asia, he received an important portion of his education in the West. Having access to a plurality of cultures is an advantage when writing a book which tries to build a bridge between such different worlds. Furthermore, the author is calmly able to combine the inspiration of an international executive teacher with that of a successful businessman, thereby adding a fundamental dimension to his testimonial and credibility. He also understands the language codes of the practicing manager.

Jagdish Parikh has been an adjunct faculty member at the International Institute for Management Development (IMD) and, for a number of years, at one of IMD's parent institutes, the International Management Institute (IMI). His book is largely derived from his pedagogical experiences during these years and the rich interaction he has had with executives from around the world. I sincerely hope to see his book as well received as his teaching has been in the classroom.

Dr Juan Rada
Director General of IMD
Lausanne, Switzerland
September 1990

Editor's Introduction

Manager Self Development
by Ronnie Lessem

Background

From Businessman to Business Yogi

For thousands of years successive Indian civilizations have developed methodologies for self-discovery, self-improvement, and self-development. Yet it is only now, in the 1990s, that an Indian businessman and social thinker, Jagdish Parikh, has applied such an approach to management. Remarkably enough, it has taken some 5000 years for this to take place.

Parikh, besides running his business in Bombay, has been Chairman of the FFC (now National Film Development Corporation of India), and Vice-Chairman of the Indian Institute for Travel and Tourism. He is President of the Indo-European Development Centre, Vice-Chairman of the World Business Academy based in the US and a governor of the Asian Institute of Management (Manila). Moreover, for the past ten years, he has been running courses on "Managing the Self," not only for multinational corporations but also for leading European management centers in Brussels, Lausanne, Stockholm and Vienna. In fact, Parikh has now also involved himself with the movement of developing and applying the "new business paradigm" principles in business around the globe.

From Professionalism to Mastery

Parikh's primary aim, over the past decade, has been to synthesize the technology of "how to make a living," based on Western expertise, with the technology of "how to live," based on Eastern philosophical traditions. The questions he therefore invites you to address are the following:

- Are you, as a manager, living for business, or are you in the business of living?
- Are you interested in adding years to your life, or life to your years?
- Is your main interest in making yourself a living, or in making a life for yourself?

In encouraging you to answer these questions to your satisfaction, through this book, Parikh is helping you to manage your thoughts, your feelings, and your emotions effectively. Moreover, in guiding you toward the management of your "consciousness," as well as your body and mind, he is constructing a bridge between West and East. In other words, by enabling you to manage your creativity and intuition, as well as your instinct and intellect, Parikh directs you beyond raw energy and professional competence towards self and managerial mastery.

From Management Principles to Managing the Self

Principles of management

For three-quarters of a century, ever since the French industrialist Henri Fayol[1] introduced the business world to his management principles, the activities of planning and organizing, directing and controlling have become strongly engrained within the conventional managerial wisdom. Some hundreds of management texts, albeit including some minor variations on this basic theme, have been written along these particular, analytically based lines. Each of the functions of business – from operations to marketing, and from finance to human resource management – have been similarly subdivided into such standardized and de-personalized activities. Finally, while basic principles of planning and control have infiltrated corporate strategy, the full panoply of management principles have beset general management and organizational behavior – with Peter Drucker providing an influential lead.[2]

Managing by wandering about

The first major break in this longstanding pattern of managerial thought and action came in the early 1980s, when Tom Peters urged managers to go back to the leadership basics.[3] In urging you and I to "manage by wandering about," keeping close to the customer, maintaining a bias for action, and adopting a hands-on, value-laden style of managerial behavior, he altered the tone but not the essence of management. For it remained an outwardly directed activity, rather than an inwardly directed one, in which the outward-looking management of people and things, rather than the inward-looking management of your self, remained the basic objective.

Manager self-development

At the same time, and particularly since the 1960s, a host of self-assessment and self-development techniques have entered the management arena. Predominant amongst these have been Eric Berne's transactional analysis of "parent," "adult," and "child",[4] geared towards self-development, and Jung's psychological types,[5] geared towards self-assessment. However, none of these have served to transform the whole of management. They have been used simply as new techniques, affecting parts of management, rather than as new paradigms, affecting the whole of management. This is where Parikh, by way of a contrast, has made his unique contribution.

The inner functions of management

Parikh, then, has shifted the entire focus of management from an outwardly directed to an inwardly directed one, aimed towards not only the manager's job but also his life as a whole. The "functions of management" are changed, then, from planning and controlling information, and organizing and directing people.

Instead, Parikh focuses on those self-directed functions of managing the body, the mind, the emotions, consciousness, and what Parikh calls the "neurosensory" system. In this introduction I shall allude briefly to each in turn.

Managing Your Self

Management of Your Body

In the West, at least after the fall of ancient Greece, there has traditionally been a separation between physical and mental activity.

segments need.

This gap is just beginning to be bridged again, in the 1990s. In the East, on the other hand, managing the physical self has always been closely connected with overall self-management, albeit in a personal rather than managerial context.

Not surprisingly, therefore, Parikh places initial emphasis on the management of the body. For the practice of yoga, so strongly entrenched within India, is based on the belief that, although the physical body is the crudest manifestation of the person:[6]

it is man's most essential principle for his growth in his present stage of development. . . . As we look around we note that the physical bodies of different individuals show different degrees of development. Some are strong, others are weak; some are lean, while others are fat. It is the duty of each developed person to train his or her body to the highest degree of perfection so that it may be used to pursue his or her spiritual purpose.

Within the Western tradition, as I have already intimated, the ancient Greek concern for "healthy body, healthy mind" has very recently been resurrected. The growing concern for health and fitness, not only amongst hard-pressed managers but also the public at large, has given rise to a whole new leisure industry.

For Parikh such "leisure" is a necessary part of work. He in fact constructs a bridge between East and West, as well as between leisure and work, by describing the part that breathing and exercise, relaxation, and diet have to play in the management of the physical self. Drawing on principles and practices of yoga from the East, and approaches to diet and nutrition from the West, he relates these to the overall management of stress, which is becoming such an important part of a manager's life. The second aspect of self with which he deals is that of mind.

Management of Your Mind

The management of your mind is more familiar, in business, than the management of your body, particularly in the light of the emergence of the so-called "knowledge worker." Edward de Bono has had a seminal influence on such "mind management," in the boardrooms of companies around the globe. A qualified physician who turned his attention to *The Mechanism of the Mind*[7] as a hobby, de Bono has since been prolific. In his best known work on *Lateral Thinking for Management*[8] he has compared and contrasted analytical, "vertical" thinking, with the more creative approach to "lateral" thinking.

More recently, Jerry Rhodes in the UK, who used to be a director of Kepner Tregoe, published his seminal work, *The Colours of Your Mind.*[9] In it he posited six different thinking styles which managers characteristically, and alternately, adopt. In a forthcoming publication for this series,[10] Rhodes will be revealing the results of the 20 years of research and development work he has been engaged in, with Philips in Holland, on managerial thinking processes.

Inevitably, as the information economy and knowledge-based organizations spread their influence, so management of the mind will become that much more important.[11]

Therefore, although the West has made the major contribution to managing the mind, recently the East has again begun to make its influence felt. In my own work on *Total Quality Learning,*[12] I have related the seven paths of yoga to a spectrum of learning styles, and of organizational fields of activity. Parikh, in his turn, compares and contrasts the analytic, scientific, and secular approach to thinking, traditionally associated with the West, to the more holistic, mystical, and spiritual approach, conventionally associated with the East. Focusing on both approaches, he indicates why and how each can be used by the thinking manager.

Managing Your Emotions

In the West in general, and in Europe in particular, much less attention has been paid to the management of the emotions than in the East, in general, and by India or Japan, in particular. Parikh points out that while we, in the West, have successfully extended our physical capacities, through transportation and mechanization, and our mental capacities through instrumentation and automation, we have hardly extended our emotional capacities at all, other than dangerously, through drugs.

In the East the practice of yoga, for example, and the martial arts is geared as much toward emotional enhancement as toward physical and mental development. The self-control required in each demands tremendous emotional discipline; in India aimed at self-realization and in Japan at social integration. In the West emotional development has been correspondingly fostered through psychotherapy, and through the so-called "personal growth" movement that began in the 1960s.

In fact, it was at this time that so-called "sensitivity training," aimed at heightening emotional sensitivity toward self and others, was imported into management. However, such "training," in contrast with Japan where the inculcation of self and social discipline is central to management, remained on the fringe of management thought and practice.

The psychotherapist who has had the most influence on "managing the self," is the late Eric Berne,[13] to whom I have already referred as as the father of so-called "transactional analysis." Parikh refers extensively to Berne's seminal work, whereby managers are enabled to manage the transactions between the "parent," the "adult," and the "child" that lives within all of them. However, Parikh maintains that the management of emotions has to be even more pervasive than that. He provides managers, therefore, with particular ways and means of managing their beliefs, their expectations, and their emotionally laden concerns.

Parikh ultimately focuses his attention on what he calls "management by detached involvement," which becomes the central, and recurring, theme of his book:

The key to success is for you to align your expectations (of results) in such a manner that your basic experience, at any given point of time, is one of satisfaction. In other words, satisfaction or happiness consists of striving to get what you want, but at the same time experiencing or wanting whatever you get.

In essence, he says, you should become involved in the activities of your work and life, in your efforts to be successful, but you should remain detached from the activities or rewards themselves.

Managing Your Neurosensory System

The fourth and most subtle dimension of yourself, according to Parikh, is what he calls the "neurosensory system," that is a combination of your nervous system and five senses.

The "information" that is distilled or filtered through your senses is your self-managed "input." This is then "processed," together with stored "data" in your memory, into thoughts, images, and beliefs. Such data processing results in an "output," that is to say your experience, at two levels. One level is internal, in your body. The other is external, in the form of your behavior. These outputs also serve, in part, as "feedback" inputs. This continuing and ongoing process of interaction, based on your neurosensory activity, is what human experience is all about.

In the context of such neurosensory activity Parikh introduces us to the left and right sides of the brain. These have in fact become a great talking point in both neurological and managerial circles since Robert Ornstein,[13] the American neuropsychologist, published his book on *The Psychology of Consciousness*. While the left side, controlling the right hand, is supposedly responsible for conceptual and analytic thinking, the right side, controlling the left hand, is responsible for holistic and contextual thought. Drawing on the power of the right brain, hitherto neglected in conventional management circles, Parikh reveals the importance of "imaging" in human and managerial activity. Through your right brain imagination you are able to picture or to literally visualize – as opposed to merely analyze – people or things.

Managing Consciousness

Finally, and drawing most explicitly on an Eastern philosophical context, Parikh deals with that ultimate managerial, and also human, concern, that of managing consciousness. In that respect he joins hands with a select band of Western physicists, of our day, most particularly the Anglo-American David Bohm,[15] who have forged new linkages between Western physical science and Eastern philosophical traditions.

While Bohm distinguishes between an "implicate" and "explicate" order of physical reality, Parikh distinguishes between implicit managerial consciousness and explicit managerial thought, feelings, and behavior, with the neurosensory system playing a mediating role.

Such layers of consciousness, seven in all, are drawn out of the energy centers identified by the Indian philosophers and mystics, upon which I have also drawn in my own managerial thinking.[16] These layers range from the more dense, that is the material or physical, to the most subtle, that is the spiritual or cosmic. Having identified these different forms of awareness, Parikh introduces us to techniques of meditation which enable us to raise our level of consciousness.

Conclusion

Both developmental management in general, and management by detached involvement in particular, are concerned with shifting the theory and practice of management toward what Parikh would call a new paradigm. In the table below, extracted from the final chapter in this book, old and new paradigms or managerial world views, are compared and contrasted:

Characteristic	Old paradigm	New paradigm
Strategy	Planned	Entrepreneurial
Structure	Hierarchy	Network
Systems	Rigid	Flexible
Staff	Title and rank	Being helpful
Style	Problem solving	Transformational
Skills	To complete	To build
Shared value	Better sameness	Meaningful difference
Focus	Institution	Individual
Source of strength	Stability	Change
Leadership	Dogmatic	Inspirational

What distinguishes Parikh's "new paradigm" book from several others, in the managerial and organizational context, is that it is concerned with not only the thinking behind organizational transformation but also with the ways and means (thinking and doing) of achieving the required personal transformation:

It is only when you operate from a detached consciousness that you can bring about authentic organizational transformation. In the process you will be transforming organizational cultures from hierarchical structures into mutual support networks, from management styles based on control and aggression to those oriented toward caring and connection. Moreover, in the final analysis, you will be transforming your role from that of either innocent or professional to that of master manager.

In the process you will be marrying up the Western "know thyself" tradition with the Eastern "become thyself" one, with more than a little help from Euro-Indian Jagdish Parikh.

Notes

1 Fayol, H., *Industrial and General Administration.* International Management Institute, 1930.
2 Drucker, P., *Management.* London: Pan, 1980.
3 Peters, T. & Waterman, R., *In Search of Excellence.* New York: Harper and Row, 1982.
4 Berne, E., *Games People Play.* New York: Grove Press, 1967.
5 Malone, M., *Psychetypes.* New York: Avon, 1974.
6 Swami Vishnudevananda, *The Complete Illustrated Book of Yoga.* London: Bell, 1959.
7 de Bono, E., *The Mechanism of Mind.* London: Penguin, 1971.
8 de Bono, E., *Lateral Thinking for Management.* London: Penguin, 1981.
9 Rhodes, J. & Thame, S., *The Colours of Your Mind.* London: Fontana, 1989.
10 Rhodes, J., *The Art of Abstraction.* Oxford: Blackwell, 1991.
11 Bennis, W. & Chenne, S., *The Planning of Change.* New York: Holt, Rinehart & Winston, 1968.
12 Lessem, R., *Total Quality Learning.* Oxford: Basil Blackwell, 1991.
13 Berne, *Games People Play.*
14 Ornstein, R., *The Psychology of Consciousness.* London: Penguin, 1974.
15 Bohm, D., *Wholeness and the Implicate Order.* London: Routledge and Kegan Paul, 1980.
16 Lessem, R., *Developmental Management.* Oxford: Blackwell, 1990.

Dedicated to my wife Shaila

Preface

This is a book written for managers who want to reach a higher level of physical, emotional, and mental well-being, and achieve a sustainably high level of performance in their personal, professional, and public lives. However, it could benefit anyone interested in enhancing and enriching his or her work and life. There are many books on this subject, which is of growing importance and relevance; and new publications are pouring in almost every day. So why write one more? I can think of a number of compelling reasons.

There is so much literature on this and related self-management topics that it is virtually impossible for a busy manager to be able to select those publications which are suitable for him, and even more so to read, digest, retain, and apply the same in his daily life. The subject itself is so vast, vague, and complex that it has not yet been presented comprehensively or in an easy to grasp manner in one book, which will enable a manager to "manage" himself efficiently and effectively in the multiple and often conflicting roles in his life.

Most of the publications are either in the "self-help" or "fitness" category (which are useful but remain at a rather shallow or symptomatic level), or are in the domain of different schools of psychology or philosophy (which are really interesting, but only for those who have a special interest at that level), or belong to a rather esoteric and sometimes even a cultist category.

In the literature on management, managers are now increasingly exposed to several concepts such as excellence, creativity, innovation, peak performance, leadership, etc. These are concepts which are undoubtedly important and of growing relevance, and there is an increasing awareness and acceptance of this. However, most of the literature does not tell us enough about how to really acquire such qualities in an authentic and durable way. Therefore, this has resulted in a significant and growing gap between what managers want to or should do and what they are actually doing or are able to do. What is needed, therefore, is the enabling knowledge, skills, and attitudes which provide the missing link between the managerial know-how, do-how, and feel-how.

In other words, what is needed is one book which at least captures and outlines the most relevant concepts and processes which enable managers to go beyond average performance and artificial behavior and acquire such qualities and inner experiences, when superior performance and the above-listed competencies become a natural consequence. It should also enable managers to contribute effectively and progressively to their organizations without in any way adversely affecting or corroding them as individuals: in fact, enabling them to lead richer, more dynamic, and increasingly more satisfying personal lives in congruence with their professional and public roles.

What is required to achieve such a mix on a sustained basis is a synthesis between the contemporary Western concepts and scientific temperament and the ancient perennial wisdom of the East as well as between conceptual and experiential approaches. This is the thrust of this book.

In the West there is a growing interest, stimulated particularly by the economic success of Japan, in an Eastern approach to management and organization. However, stress is killing an increasing number of Japanese, particularly Japanese businessmen: they call it "karoshi" (death from overwork) or "pokkuri byo" (sudden death). There is therefore a need to understand the nature of the missing link between contemporary and emerging Japanese business culture and the authentic and perennial Eastern wisdom – between yen and zen!

Being an Indian, I have a background in Eastern tradition and Indian culture. My basic education was at a school with a strong Gandhian slant, and my college education was very much in the British tradition. In addition, I have the benefit of having been educated at Harvard Business School in the USA. Then, for over 25 years, I have been involved with business, government, and education. I have been a successful entrepreneur and businessman in India. In addition to being an "owner–manager" in many private-sector businesses, I have headed a public-sector corporation, and several industrial and cultural associations. I have also been a member of formative and policy-making bodies of management schools, as well as a member of the teaching faculty. These opportunities have helped me to synthesize the Western and Eastern, modern and ancient, conceptual and experiential, and to ground this "amalgam" at the level of managerial practice. I believe that it is such a synthesis that will facilitate the emergence of a new paradigm in organizational cultures and managerial styles.

Finally, as a visiting professor at several international management schools, I have initiated and developed a program on "Managing the Self," which is becoming more popular every year, particularly because of its conceptual soundness and practical realism. This program has been developed not only on the basis of the conceptual knowledge that I have acquired through my cultural background and special study but, more importantly, on the basis of my personal and practical experience in trying these concepts out in the various roles of my own life, in both the East and the West.

It is in the above perspective that I have attempted this book. I am fully aware that no one book can really provide all the answers (including this one). However, this is an effort to provide as comprehensive coverage of the most critical areas in self management as possible, in as simple and as practical a manner as possible. I have therefore used as many schematic diagrams and tables as possible to enable several abstract and complex concepts and processes to be understood easily. A picture, it is said, conveys more than a thousand words: a diagram is supposed to express more than a few pictures. However, I have presented them as aids to understanding and not as theoretical models. I have deliberately resisted the temptation to make this book more detailed or scholarly. At the same time, I have kept in mind Albert Einstein's famous quote "Make things as simple as possible, but not any simpler."

It is in the context of the changing international perspectives, contemporary management thinking, personal convictions based on insight and experience, and teaching success, that I have set out to write this book. It is an effort to build a management bridge between East and West, and also to present basic concepts and processes on managing your self in as comprehensive, and yet as simple and practical, a manner as possible. I hope this will help you to manage your work and life in a way that enables you to do more and feel better! People who feel good within themselves generally bring about better results on a sustained basis.

Throughout the book the generic pronoun 'he' is used. This usage is not gender specific.

Jagdish Parikh

Acknowledgements

I have learnt most of what I have expressed in this book from several people whom I have read, heard, and met. I had never intended to write such a book. Unfortunately, therefore, I have not kept any record of the sources of several rich ideas and processes included in this book, which is largely an amalgam of what I have learnt from others. My most sincere regret is that I am unable to acknowledge individually such contributions, except for a few which I have mentioned.

I would like to express my deep gratitude to Dr Juan Rada for his considerate Foreword; to Dr Alden Lank, Dr Fred Neubauer, Dr Michael Royston, Jean Louis Servan-Schreiber; and to Dr Ronnie Lessem for encouraging me by perusing the manuscript and offering valuable suggestions.

This book would not have been possible without the ongoing supportive energy from my family. I am therefore deeply indebted to:

my parents
for cultivating and nurturing my "inner core"; My father, Natverlal, for developing my rational and philosophical interests and insights; My mother, Chandrakala, for artistic, creative and emotional sensibilities.

my children
Prashant and Anuradha for encouraging and enriching my ideas and concepts with well-informed suggestions and stimulating discussions.

my brothers
Arvind and Pranav for their affectionate and generous support and facilitating the necessary freedom for me to pursue this project outside my family business responsibilities.

The delightful cartoons were executed by Mr V. Halbe.

Introduction

The title *Managing Your Self* may intrigue you. For many people, the essence of good management is "objectivity:" decisions and actions based on "objective" data to achieve corporate objectives. From that perspective, "managing your self" may appear to be neither relevant nor even desirable.

However, such a feeling results from an inappropriate understanding of both the terms "management" and "self." In the first place there is no single, universally accepted definition of management. Every manager has his own unique perception and orientation about management. "Management" in that sense, to a large extent, lies in the eye of the beholder, and each beholder is influenced by his status, personality, and culture. Secondly, although one of the most frequently used words in any manager's vocabulary is "I" or "me" or "myself," if you were asked to specify what you meant when using such expressions, you would probably experience confusion and discomfort in articulating what your "self" is.

These very uncertainties regarding "self" and "management" represent a major barrier, inhibiting you from realizing your full potential and achieving peak performance. I consider management as a process through which you become deeply aware of and facilitate full development of that which you are managing, creating a context in which managment happens and performance peaks. This book therefore aims to make good managers better. It should enable you to be aware of, and access, your deeper potential, enhancing your self-entrepreneurship. It should help you to reach and sustain peak performance, improve your leadership qualities, and even empower you to transform organizations.

Stress is not Beautiful!

The origin of this book can be traced back to the time, several years ago when, fresh from India, I entered Harvard Business School, not fully aware what awaited me there. Needless to say, I did not have to wait long to find out. The Dean made that quite clear during the welcoming address, which came through to me as follows:

Two years to obtain a Masters degree in Business Administration may seem like a long time right now. But, I assure each and everyone of you that it will ultimately seem too short. The MBA program is designed to ensure that there will always be much more work to be done everyday than the time and energy you have at your disposal. Each day you will be given at least 8 hours of homework, despite the fact that you will have hardly 4 hours to do it in. This is deliberately planned with two objectives: to bring you closer to the real business world in which you will always have more problems to solve than your available resources; and also to create pressure on you to get 8 hours work done in 4 hours. Such stress will bring the best out of you!

To me the message that came across was that *stress is beautiful*. That raised a fundamental question in my mind, which underlies this book: Is stress really necessary to bring the best out of us? But before I could begin to reflect on this, the Dean said something which created an even deeper conflict in me:

Harvard is internationally famous, not only for the form and content of its MBA program but also for its system of continual student performance evaluation and grading. This system is comprehensive, rigorous, and objective; but the ultimate judgements are based on the human element. Hence, errors are likely to occur and you may occasionally get good grades! But never feel satisfied or content with whatever you have achieved, because the moment you do so, your progress will stop, as your drive for achieving more, and doing better will get dampened.

This disturbed me even more as it conflicted directly with the value system I had grown up with. I had been brought up with a belief that for all practical purposes, this is the only life we have and that it is also a short one. We have therefore to make the best of every moment of it. *We have to try to experience, during each and every moment of our existence, the maximum possible satisfaction and contentment with whatever we have or with whatever we have achieved.*

There is, of course, an essential precondition. We have to ensure, honestly and sincerely, that we have made the maximum possible effort toward achieving whatever tasks, objectives, or goals we may have set for ourselves. But as far as the results are concerned, we have to accept them with equanimity, for such results depend on a variety of external factors and variables over which we do not have full control.

What the Dean of HBS was recommending seemed to me to be in direct contradiction to such an approach. He made me wonder why I had to be dissatisfied with my present achievement in order to strive towards a "higher" level of future achievement. He seemed to imply that if I am at point "A" and want to "progress" to point "B," then I have to be dissatisfied at point "A," so that I would conjure up the necessary effort, according to this logic, to move toward point "B." Assuming that I reached point "B," then the same process would need to be repeated to reach point "C," and so on. The implication was that if I was to "progress" continually in my life, I would continually remain dissatisfied. If this is the approach and its consequence, then what is the purpose of life? What is the meaning of progress? What price progress? Perhaps, I began to reflect, it is such an approach that underlies the intense stress, tension, and consequent illness that prevail in the contemporary business world.

Although these questions remained unanswered at that time, they lay festering in my mind. True to the Dean's words, the stress level throughout the MBA program remained persistently high, leaving no time for me to resolve such basic philosophical doubts over the meaning of work and life. In fact, as a result of the intensive experience of those two years, I became a typical Harvard "product."

After securing the much coveted MBA degree I returned to India, entered the family business with great ambitions and, under the influence of my Harvard mentors *stressed myself into success*. My admiration for Harvard, and especially the Dean, increased considerably; for HBS (or so it seemed to me at the time) had successfully created, in the curriculum and classroom, an environment typical of the "real" business world. The entire fabric of business was indeed based on wanting more than you had. I therefore felt that I would always remain indebted to HBS for teaching me how to succeed in such a business culture, and thereby how to make a living.

The constant and compelling drive within me to do more, and to do it better, enabled me to achieve such "progress and success" during the first few years. However, I noticed that in the process I had developed symptoms of severe stress. This caused me great anxiety. If this was my psycho-physiological state at this young age and stage of my life, what would happen during the rest of my life? The doubts and conflicts that had assailed me that very first day at Harvard re-emerged. This time I asked myself with renewed vigor: Is stress necessary to bring the best out of me? Is dissatisfaction necessary in order to achieve progress? I looked around and noticed that most of my colleagues, very competent and "successful" businessmen, also had similar stress symptoms.

Moreover, there was something wrong, something missing. I took a long, hard look this time and realized that these executives and businessmen had somehow confined themselves to very limited interests in life – they had narrowed themselves down as human beings. Most of them were neither really happy nor healthy. Despite the fact that they were exceptionally capable businessmen, most of them had developed hardly a fraction of their full human potential. They were "successful" people in the conventional sense but to me, at a deeper level, they were more like "success fools." I realized that I too was becoming one of them!

At this stage it was quite clear to me that I did not want to continue to be such a "successful executive." I wondered how I could achieve further progress, higher performance, and success in business, *without stress and with satisfaction*. These reflections led to much self-searching and to further deliberations on issues fundamental to management, to business, and to life itself.

Success and Satisfaction can Co-exist

An integral part of my search was a study that I had undertaken on "managerial attitudes, performance, and satisfaction." It had earned me a doctorate, but more importantly than that, I had begun to discover that with a certain combination of knowledge, skill, and attitude, success could be achieved with satisfaction and without stress. Success and stress need not co-exist, whereas success and satisfaction can. You could be successful without being a "success fool" if you "managed" your "self" in a certain way, in a more "professional" manner.

What I realized is that you need to apply the same analytical approach that a professional manager uses in managing an organization to the management of your own self or life. In other words, you need to explicitly set up your life goals and objectives, and adopt appropriate policies and strategies to guide your daily pursuits in alignment with, and within the perspective of, your environment and goals. This involves developing a vision and adopting appropriate strategies, as well as planning, organizing, implementing, controlling, and evaluating your own life and work, in dynamic and growing organizations.

In this way, as I have found, you can maximize the return on investment on your life. The most precious and nonrenewable resource you possess is time: every day, every moment that passes, has gone forever, and with every passing moment there are fewer moments left in your life. It is therefore vital that you derive the maximum possible "return," or "units of satisfaction," from each moment, both physically and psychologically.

Achieving Congruence

What is the relevance of such self-management to a business corporation the main objective of which is to enhance its "bottom line"? All management theories and models are ultimately focused on improving the performance of both individuals and organizations in order to achieve that. Therefore, anything that enhances individual or organizational performances is relevant to business corporations.

In recent times, managers have increasingly come to realize that while it is important to develop appropriate structures, systems, styles, and skills within an organization to enhance performance, you cannot generalize or standardize them. Each organization is, in some sense, different from the others. Therefore, there has been an increasing emphasis on the need to articulate the organization's *purpose* (why it exists – its ideology), *vision* (what it needs to do in order to achieve its purpose – its philosophy), and *strategy* (how it is going to implement this – its technology). In other words, the structure and systems of an organization should be such that they facilitate its purpose, vision, and strategy so that performance is maximized. Of course, all the other resources of manpower, money, and materials have to be provided to make up the whole corporate performance, as shown in Figure 1.1.

Similarly, in the past few years, it has been emphasized that corporate purpose, vision, and strategy cannot be formulated in isolation. They have to take into account the "external environment," including economic, technological, political, and social forces. Unless these variables are taken into account in the formulation of the

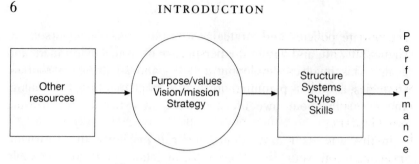

Figure 1.1 Performance Elements.

corporate purpose, vision, and strategy (and also in its structure, systems, styles, and skills), optimum performance cannot be achieved (see Figure 1.2).

It is only very recently that one more variable has been added to the above model, namely, *the internal environment* of the organization: its unique *culture*, the quality and character of the interaction amongst the individuals and groups or teams. The significance and crucial

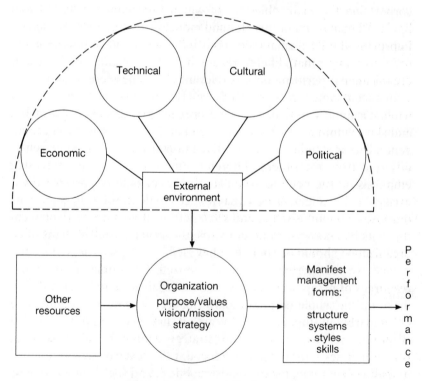

Figure 1.2 External Environment.

relevance of this internal variable is being increasingly emphasized in contemporary management theory and practice. Ultimately, however, the internal culture of any organization depends on the individual selves within the organization and their mind-sets, or their thinking, feeling, and behavior.

A complete performance model would therefore be the one shown in Figure 1.3. You have to align the internal culture, external environment, corporate purpose, vision, and strategy and the managerial structure, systems, styles, and skills so as to empower the organization to achieve peak performance.

In this context, it is important to note that any organization has to be extremely careful to achieve what I would call a "strategic congruence" between strategy and internal culture (see Figure 1.4). There are usually a variety of alternative strategies that any organization can pursue (such as A, B, C, or D). Similarly, there are a variety of internal cultures (such as 1, 2, 3, or 4). For any strategy to be effective on a sustainable basis, there has to be a congruence, or fit, between the strategy and the internal culture. Organizations have frequently found that, even though they may have chosen the most appropriate strategy after elaborate studies and deliberations, somehow these strategies have either failed or not succeeded to the expected level or over the expected period.

This is particularly so today, when corporate strategies have to change rapidly in response to environmental change, thereby requiring the internal culture also to change. To change the internal culture is not easy because, as I have implied, the organizational culture reflects the interaction amongst its individuals, each one of which is a unique entity (see Figure 1.5). These cannot be altered so easily or rapidly – unless a special effort is made and expertise developed to manage one's self, one's beliefs, and one's behaviors, in a manner that enhances the "specialness" of every individual as well as intensifying a meaningful "commonness" within the organisation.

Managing Your Self

It is the corporation's objective then, in managing all of its "selves," to enable individuals to consciously reflect on, sort out, and take positions on the "why" (philosophy), "what" (ideology), and "how" (strategy) of their lives. It is this individual and collective process in an organization that creates "attunement" within and among the

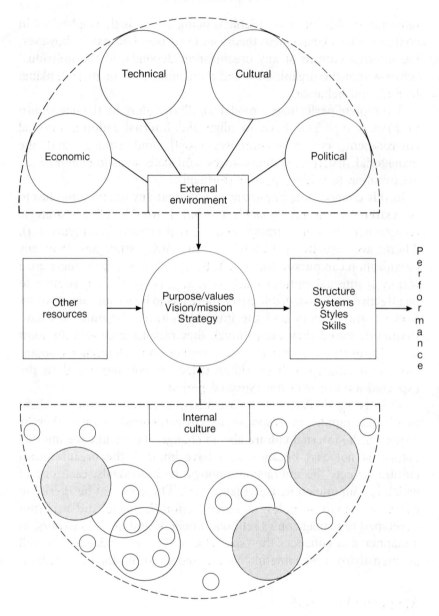

Figure 1.3 Integrated Performance.

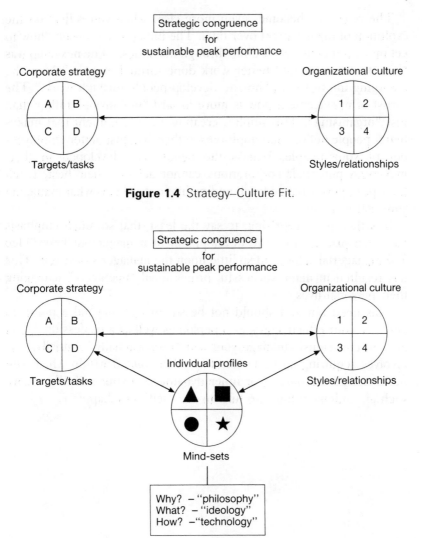

Figure 1.4 Strategy–Culture Fit.

Figure 1.5 Corporate Empowerment.

individuals, facilitates "alignment" between the internal culture and the corporate strategy, and thereby generates the required degree of "empowerment," so that individual and corporate performance can be enhanced on a sustained basis. Unless the individual instruments are in harmony with each other in an orchestra, the result would be noise and not music. This is the relevance of managing the self for any organization.

The relevance becomes even more clear when you reflect on the evolution of management over time. The initial focus was on "how to get more and better work done through machines." The next step was "how to get more and better work done through people." Now the emerging interest is in "how to develop people through work." The thrust of management now is more toward "mobilising" rather than just "organising". This implies creating an environment that makes better people out of your employees, rather than just better employees out of your people. Unless the people are developed to their maximum potential, corporations cannot achieve their best, reach their peak performance level, and maintain it. This is what managing your self is about.

It is therefore surprising, to say the least, that so much emphasis has been placed upon the development of management knowledge and managerial skills, and so little upon the manager's own self. This has resulted in many successful professional "managers" damaging their personal lives.

This need not and should not be so. In fact, beyond a point, to enhance your effectiveness as a person as well as a professional, you have to consciously manage your self "professionally." Initially, this involves acquiring an understanding of the *context* within which you function and the *content*, or inner dynamics, of your self. To secure such an understanding, we turn to the "self" in Chapter 1.

PART I

Your Self

I

Levels of Self

The Context: Five Levels of Existence

As a human entity, every manager exists at five different (but not mutually exclusive) levels:

1 as a citizen at the level of *society*;
2 as a member of the *organization* in which he works;
3 as a *manager* within the organization, with specific responsibilities and resources;
4 as a *person* involved in multiple roles involving family, job, and community;
5 at the level of "being" which is often referred to as the *existential* level.

Inherent in each level are issues which concern us all as managers, and which we have to cope with. Unless we take a clear position on such macro-issues, or at least be aware of them and in some cases accept them as unresolved, we are likely to carry with us layers of avoidable anxiety and uncertainty. These inevitably act as barriers to our personal growth as well as professional performance.

Some of the basic issues that have emerged in our contemporary environment at these different levels are as follows.

1 *The societal level* Science, technology, and management have made a rising standard of living possible, particularly in the past few decades, as measured by economic indices. However, it is also generally recognized, although it has not yet been made sufficiently explicit that, at an individual or personal level, life has become increasingly tense and pressured. This growing amount of stress

and psychophysical illness has resulted in a gradual lowering of the quality of life, from a psychosocial perspective. The accelerating pace and complexity of change, together with the growing amount of conflict and tension at global, regional, and national levels, further reinforce this concern, and the resultant search for better ways of living.

2 *The organizational level*   In the light of these rapid and complex changes, organizations are engaged in a search for more relevant and congruent cultures, strategies, and leadership profiles. This calls for the cultivation of a mix of qualities and competencies in managers that is very different from the conventional ones of planning, directing, organizing, and controlling. In fact, many of the traditional management programs are yielding diminishing returns in terms of incremental managerial performance.

3 *The managerial level*   There is a growing feeling amongst managers, as Warren Bennis says, that they are overmanaged and underled. Moreover, specialization has facilitated not only standardization but also alienation, disposability, and diminishing job satisfaction. In this context, for the individual manager following a course of "management by objectives," the question increasingly arises as to whose objectives – corporate or personal – are being attained? While there need not and should not be any divergence between these two aspects, unfortunately there is normally considerable (and avoidable) conflict between them.

4 *The personal level*   Apart from a general undercurrent of "stress-flation," several managers, particularly the more mature, upper level, and "successful" ones, do come to ask questions such as: What is all this about? What is going on around me and in my life? Am I personally really getting all that I am working for and seeking in this high-pressure and constantly demanding life, which involves multiple roles and conflicts both at work and at home? Am I burning myself out too fast? Do I, at this stage, really have any other choices? Such questions become more intense and frustrating, particularly for those managers who tend to think far ahead, even toward their retirement, although it may still be far away.

The more aware and sensitive managers then begin to seriously review their life styles and life gains. How might they secure continuing advancement in their careers, harmony in their families, and maximum personal growth, thereby combining minimum stress with maximum satisfaction?

While a large number of managers have these desires, many of them are unsure as to what is the best way to achieve what seems like a rather ambitious and complex objective. Moreover, most of them seem to think that they have hardly any discretionary time or energy for thinking through such issues. It is always easier to ride the horse in the direction in which it is going!

5 *The existential level* Some of the most fundamental unresolved issues remain at this level. Unfortunately, these tend to be the least understood or attended. They relate to concepts such as freedom, isolation, death, and the meaning or purpose of life itself.

These five levels of your existence and their attendant issues and concerns, or challenges and opportunities, form the context of your self. Moreover, all of the activities in these levels can be structured or classified within four major roles – job, family, community, and your own self. See Figure 1.6.

To cope with the demands that one faces in these five levels and from these four roles, nature has endowed us with almost unlimited potential. This potential can be divided into five rich dimensions, which form the content of your self.

The Content: Five Dimensions of Your Self

What is self? Until someone asks, you seem to know. When you want to explain, you do not know! If you were asked who or what is it that you are referring to when you use the word "I," what would be your response? Most people find it rather difficult and even uncomfortable to articulate a clear response to such a question. It is beyond intellectual comprehension and verbal articulation. If you have to describe, even in detail, the organization in which you have been working for a few years, it would be relatively easy to do so; but when it comes to describing your own self, the "organization" inside your skin, with which you have been living all your life, you often feel surprisingly incapable.

In order to gain a better feeling or understanding of what your self is and what it is not, let us consider a dialogue. If I ask you "Whose shirt is it that you are wearing?" you would say "It is mine." That implies that you are the owner, user, and experiencer of your shirt.

You are thereby implying or confirming that you are not the shirt. Whatever is yours is not you, almost by definition. Subject and object cannot be the same at the same time. Pursuing this further, if I ask you "Whose body is this on which you are wearing this shirt?" your response would naturally be "It is my body." This would indicate that you have a body (just as you have a shirt), but that you are not the body. This would stimulate some thoughts in you as to what I am driving at, and if I were now to ask you "Whose thoughts are those which you are now experiencing?" you would again say "Mine."

Therefore, you are neither your thoughts nor your mind: you are the experiencer of both. This realization might generate some discomfort. If you are not your body or your mind, then what else are you? Whose feeling is this that you are now experiencing? Again, it is your feeling – you are not your feeling or your emotion. You *have* a body, mind, and emotions, but you *are* none of these. The persistent conflicts that you experience in your life and work are largely due to this mistaken identity that you give yourself. In fact, you could take this even further and affirm that your name is not you: it is a label or identification given to you at birth by others.

It is not the "I" but the "me" that we know and identify with. The eye can see other things but not itself; the finger tip can touch other objects but not itself. What I am suggesting is that your self is not your body, mind, or emotions: these are some of the aspects or dimensions or, shall we say, functional areas of your self.

The remaining two more subtle dimensions of the self are what have been described as the "neurosensory system" and "states of consciousness."

Functions of Self

Pursuing the analogy of management of a business organization through functional areas such as marketing, finance, production, human resources, research and development, etc., you could consider these five dimensions of the self – body, mind, emotion, neurosensory system, and consciousness – as the functional areas of the self. To enable effective management or your self, as in the case of a business organization, you have to develop special awareness and expertise for each of these functional areas, or self dimensions. This is, in a sense, a "selfing" technology. Unless you develop it and you consciously manage your self, someone else will! This is what *Managing Your Self* is about.

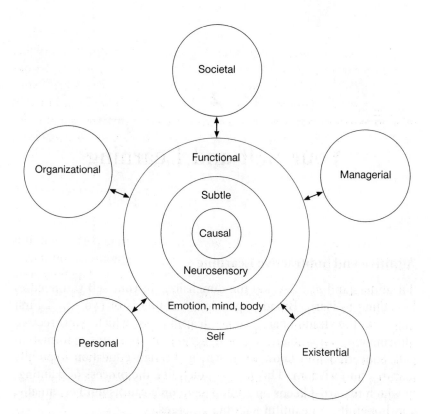

Figure 1.6 Managing Your Self: Levels and Dimensions.

2

Your Self and Learning

Additive and Subtractive Learning

To understand *and* develop the dimensions of your self you need to be willing to learn. Broadly speaking, learning is of two types. First there is the traditional *additive* learning in which you receive information sequentially. Over a period of time this information gets converted into knowledge, which through education hopefully matures into wisdom. This is very much like the process of painting, in which the artist keeps on adding paint on a canvas until eventually, and hopefully, a beautiful painting emerges.

However, after a certain age and stage in your life, the developing manager has to use another type of learning, which is *subtractive* and is analogous to sculpting. Over a period of time, you will have accumulated a certain body of knowledge, and acquired various beliefs and attitudes. Several of these, in fact, may have become obsolete or may function as barriers to your growth. These need to be identified and chiselled out – and, as in sculpting, after chiselling out the junk, a beautiful sculpture emerges. Unless you are willing and open to objectively review and, when necessary, alter your mental or emotional constructs, there cannot be any real learning or growth.

Another way of looking at your general attitude toward learning is to ask yourself how much of your existing knowledge you are actually "using" in your life. Most of us use hardly a fraction; and yet our constant endeavor is to acquire even more. Imagine someone in a business organization suggesting a major addition to the installed plant capacity when its utilization is less than 10 percent! In such a situation, the entire resources and energies of the organization would be focused on increasing the utilization of the existing capacity, rather than adding to it. Similarly, it might perhaps be beneficial to explore ways and means of enhancing the use of what you already know, while also continuing your search for more knowledge.

This is a crucial issue, because most managers find that there is a significant gap between what they know (volume A) and how much they use (volume B) (and, more importantly, use effectively – level C). This is illustrated in Figure 2.1.

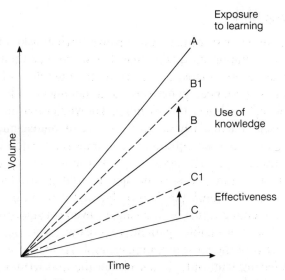

Figure 2.1 Learning Effectiveness.

There are an increasing number of "models" being published currently, illustrating "the profile of a superior manager," "leadership qualities," "creativity," "excellence," "organization transformation" and so on. And yet, because of the chronic and continuing missing link between knowledge or expertise and behavior or performance, knowledge does not automatically become converted into *performance*. It remains more of an inventory, not value added. Therefore this proliferation of models, while providing intellectual stimulation and a degree of psychological satisfaction, has not resulted in raising significantly the levels of excellence in most managers or organizations. In fact, it contributes to the level of frustration amongst those aspiring managers who feel they are not "making a real difference," despite their enhanced knowledge and training. Acquiring knowledge is not the same thing as applying it: knowing more does not necessarily lead to behaving differently. In business, knowledge by itself is not power. Although our society is described as an information society, we are still an ignorant society!

This is not to imply that one should not pursue knowledge. I only emphasize the need to develop appropriate skills and attitudes as well, to enhance the use and effectiveness curve B toward B1 and curve C toward C1, respectively, in Figure 2.1.

The Missing Link

In a recent survey with which I was involved, when asked to identify one single most important quality that they would like their bosses to have, almost every manager referred to qualities of fairness, understanding, patience, generosity, and openness. All these are humane, caring qualities, not so much knowledge-based but more behavior-based. Particularly at upper levels of management, while knowledge and expertise continue to be important, such behavioral qualities acquire a greater signficance. These are the qualities that our subordinates and peers would like to find in us. How do we acquire or cultivate them? The knowledge that you should have such qualities is not enough. Just by knowing, or even consciously deciding to become fair, reasonable, patient, or creative, you do not really become so. One of the most revealing examples is that of speaking the truth, or behaving truthfully. It is said that the first written record of behaving truthfully as a basic code of human conduct was found in 8000 BC when there were only 5 million human inhabitants on Earth. Even now, in almost AD 2000, that is 10,000 years later, when we are more than 5 billion on Earth, all civilized cultures still advocate truthfulness – and this has been the case throughout this period, during which 50 billion people have lived and died. But despite this knowledge and desire to be truthful, are we (truthfully) more truthful today than they were in 8000 BC?

What is this missing link – the "causal" factor or the blocking barrier – between desire and ability? To help you answer the question, let me tell you a couple of stories.

There was a man called Nasruddin who, one late dark evening, was frantically searching for something on the roadside under a street light. One of his friends who was passing by asked him "What are you searching for?" Nasruddin replied that he had lost the key to his house. His friend joined him in the search, but after some time, not yet finding the key, asked "Nasir, can you remember where you might have dropped the key?" The reply was prompt: "Of course I do, I dropped it in front of my house, way out there." The friend asked, "Then why are you searching here?" Nasruddin replied "This is the only place where I can see under the street light!"

Another story is about a person who was throwing breadcrumbs on a busy street corner. On being asked as to why he was doing such a strange thing, he replied by saying that in this way he was keeping "the tigers away." On being told that there were no tigers in that area, he responded "Doesn't that prove that what I am doing is most effective?"

The moral of these stories is that we have to search for the "missing link" in the right place, and review our current behavior with an open mind, unblocked by preconceived notions.

One of the major barriers in this is our scientific temperament. We have been brought up and educated in a system dominated by classical physics which stipulates that "seeing is believing:" we conveniently ignore the fact that there are frequently optical illusions, such as the mirage on the highway on a hot sunny afternoon. We "see" water on the horizon although in reality it is not there. Similarly, while observing a fast rotating fan, we do not see any blades, although the blades are there. In fact, at a certain speed we see the rotation of the fan in a direction *opposite* to what it actually is.

Believing is Seeing

To understand, appreciate, and experience some of the "learnings" from the so called "nonscientific" disciplines, you have to adopt an opposite attitude; namely, "believing is seeing." For example, if I were to ask, showing my empty left hand, "Is there music in my left hand?" the obvious response would be negative, as no one can "hear" any music from my hand. However, upon placing a small transistor radio in my left hand, switching it on, and tuning it to a particular channel, you could hear some music. Is the music created by the radio, or is it only transmitted by it? You could place this radio anywhere else in the room, or in another room or another building, another city or another country, and hear the same music depending upon the power of the transmission and the radio transistors.

The point is that "music" (or "information") is all over the area covered by the broadcasting transmitter. The radio merely converts or transforms the sound waves into a range which the human ear can perceive or experience. There is a general *belief* about this, and therefore people use the radio or TV, switch it on, and tune it into the appropriate or preferred channel. So, you believe, you do the required things so that you see or experience. The well known phenomenon of the placebo effect reinforces this argument. If the patient believes that he is taking a curative medicine, even though he is actually being given a placebo, he does get cured. This has been observed in a significant number of experiments. "Believing is seeing"! This is a necessary prelude to understanding and experiencing some of the concepts and processes derived from Eastern disciplines to which we shall be exposed in later chapters. In this context, "nonscience" is not "nonsense!"

You now have the preliminary background about your self and your approach to learning to move purposefully toward self mastery. That is what we shall pursue in the next chapter.

3

Toward Self Mastery

Overcoming Dissonance

We can now begin to apply a professional approach to management of our selves, or our lives, starting at the most practical or fundamental level.

What do you want from life, or from your self? In other words, what is the objective of your self? The usual responses from managers to such questions are: wealth, health, power, success, happiness, family harmony, and satisfaction.

The responses to the question "What is it that you usually get most of the time in your activity, as a manager?" are usually: frustration, anger, problems, stress, satisfaction, and excitement.

While most managers maintain that they experience negative feelings for more than 50 percent of the time, some experience the opposite. Nevertheless, there seems to be a consensus that, irrespective of the actual ratio, they would like to reduce the negative experiences and enhance the positive ones.

When I probed further with those managers who indicated that they wanted wealth, health, or power, I found that it was happiness or satisfaction that they were really seeking through these mediating factors. Moreover, ironically, as their responses indicated, their "satisfaction" had not increased despite their acquisition of more wealth or power. In other words, most managers, even the most successful ones, had less in the way of positive feelings of satisfaction than they wanted, despite their higher level of success.

Why should this be so? Why does "success" often not yield happiness, despite the fact that whatever we identify as success is ultimately sought to yield satisfaction? One of the reasons is that in the process of achieving success, and pursuing it in the various roles you have to play in your life, you have to undertake several things which you do not like to, but which you have to do. Unfortunately, in contemporary life this happens to a significant extent (see Figure 3.1).

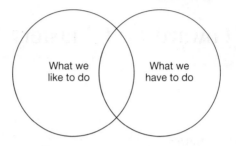

Figure 3.1 The Dissonance Factor.

This dissonance creates a lot of stress and frustration. To be able to reduce it, or maximize the overlap between what you have to do and what you like to do, thereby maximizing satisfaction, is one of the main aims of managing your self.

Beyond the Peter Principle

Another possible reason for poor self-management is the widely held belief that sooner or later we will reach our level of incompetence: this is also called "plateauing." There is a strong conviction, illustrated in Figure 3.2, that everyone goes through a growth period (A) which is followed by a stable, or stagnant, period (B). This marks the "plateauing" phase which, in turn, is followed by a decline (C). It appears that this endless cycle of birth, growth, stagnation, decay, and death is characteristic of all forms of individual and institutional life.

The prospect of plateauing, and then of decline, haunts career executives who have been in the same job for 10–15 years. Most of them see themselves as being between points B and C. Feelings of uncertainty and fear that they may have reached the plateau, or are on their way down, are not uncommon amongst managers in mid-career: the plateau is seen as inevitable. The growing complexity and demands on performance placed on them by the organization, in a contemporary environment of accelerating change, accumulates to such an extent that it makes them feel that in the not too-distant

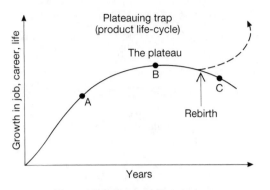

Figure 3.2 Beyond Plateauing.

future, they will reach a stage when they will no longer be able to respond to these demands effectively. This naturally results in frustration, fear, insecurity, and stress. Such feelings are by no means confined to people at points B and C – they occasionally assail people even at position A.

What we do not realize, or what a lot of us are not aware of, is that there is a way out of this apparently inevitable trap, by creating a perceptual change in our attitudes and belief systems. You can, at any stage in the cycle of your life be "reborn" (psychologically). You can "renew" yourself. Not only is this possible, but there exists the possibility of perpetual renewal in virtually every aspect of our lives through a perceptual process of rebirth. This requires a fresh look at the inner potential that each one of us possesses.

We narrow down the possibilities in our lives by having an extremely limited awareness of our true potential, which is, for all practical purposes, unlimited. On the basis of such ignorance, we limit our ambitions or aspirations, and because of our strong belief in our "inadequacies" or "limitations," almost as a self-fulfilling prophecy, we program ourselves into a very limited performance.

Our concept of "what we can do" is, to begin with, very limited. Within such a limited concept, we determine "what we want/should do;" and ultimately what we are "able" to do is only a fraction of this, as shown in Figure 3.3.

It is the convergence of what we "want" to do, together with what we feel in our hearts that we "should" do, with what we are actually "able" to do that yields the experience of "joy" or "satisfaction" see Figure 3.4.

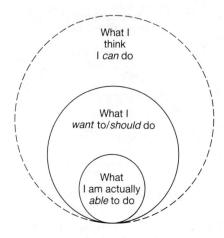

Figure 3.3 Self "Imposed" Limits.

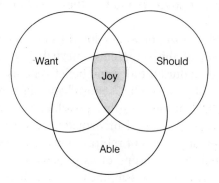

Figure 3.4 The Realm of Joy.

Tapping your Human Potential

The first step, therefore, is for you to become aware of your real potential in all aspects and dimensions of your self and then to enhance the same. An outline of these parameters is given in Table 3.1.

While, for instance, in your normal life you do not need to discriminate between 8 million shades of colors or between 300,000 different tones, the information given in Table 3.1 indicates the range of potential to which you have access. In other words, you need not continue to harbor the belief, and the consequent fear, of experiencing stagnation in your competences or capacities.

Table 3.1 Human potential

Aspect	System	Capabilities
Physical	Senses	Eyes: can discriminate 8 million shades
		Ears: can discriminate 300,000 tones
	Muscles	When all 600 pinpointed, can pull 25 tons
	Bone	One cubic inch can stand 2 tons force
Mental	Brain	Super-computer with immense observing, recording, analyzing, recalling, and storing capacity equivalent to thousands of contemporary mainframes Beyond computing, it has almost immeasurable learning, understanding imaging, creative, and intuitive abilities
Emotional		Range of feelings
Neurosensory		Multisensory/intersensory capacity
Consciousness		Spectrum of fields and levels

Beyond Categories: The "Seed" Principle

Several models of "human classifications" or "personality types" are prevalent today, a few of which are illustrated in Table 3.2.

Table 3.2 Human classifications

Classification	Authors	Descriptors
Personality type	Friedman and Roseman	"A" or "B"
Personality type	Jungian/Myers-Brigg	Extrovert/introvert Sensing/intuitive Thinking/feeling Judging/perceiving
Orientation	Blake and Mouton	Task/people grid
Need hierarchy	Maslow	Physiological/sociological/ psychological/transpersonal
Life positions	Eric Berne	I'm OK/I'm not OK
Ego states	Eric Berne	Parent/adult/child

All of these, and other, classifications or categories can be very useful in making us aware of our predominant characteristics or orientations. Unfortunately, however, with such "typing" we are frequently left with a feeling that we are in one mold, or category, and have to live with it. In fact, in many organizations "teams" or "task forces" are formed on the basis of such classifications. This supposedly serves to ensure that all the qualities and competences that are required in the performance of any project or task are provided for by this grouping and balancing of different personality types in a team. This can be beneficial in that it may well lead to higher team performance up to a point. But, unless some conscious "balancing" training is given to each team member, to cultivate his or her less dominant characteristics or traits, that person is likely to be permanently blocked or locked in that limited "track," through such constant reinforcements at work.

It is therefore important to realize that, keeping in mind the almost unlimited human potential that you are gifted with in all your dimensions, you can change, evolve, blossom, and grow into a fuller, greater, richer human being (see Figure 3.5). You can change – if you really want to.

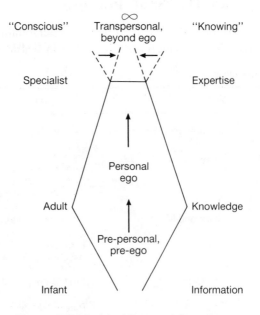

Figure 3.5 Model of Personal Growth.

The central point of this "personal growth" model is that you, as a human being, are like a "seed" with a tremendous amount of dormant potential. You have a choice: either feel the "comfort" or "security" of remaining a "seed" all your life or take a more dynamic courageous attitude, and fertilize and nurture the seed. Then you will enable the "seed" to break through its "barriers," and blossom through various evolutionary stages into a fully grown plant or tree, with all the richness of its flowers or fruits. From childhood you grow into adulthood and aspire to be a specialist, by converting information to knowledge and then to expertise, through primary, secondary, and advanced education. At this stage you have built up your "personal ego," based on several learnt beliefs and identities. You now have two choices. You can restrict your future growth by remaining like a seed that is trapped in the "box" of your restrictive beliefs or ego state. Alternatively, you may choose to "believe" in the possibilities of breaking through such psychological barriers into a different, higher, domain of existence, by cultivating a special expertise (knowledge plus skills plus attitudes) by converting work ethic into a growth ethic. This involves gaining access to and experiencing higher levels of consciousness and going beyond ego, thereby opening up alternative, but hitherto dormant, channels of knowing. This is what "managing your self" is about.

The Master Manager: "Re-visioning"

Broadly speaking, managers can be classified into three categories; (a) The innocent manager, (b) The learned manager, and (c) The master manager (see Figure 3.6).

Prior to the development of management as a profession and a distinct educational discipline, most executives managed their business organizations through their commonsense and personal insights. If you operate at this level, you are an "innocent manager."

However, as the functions of business and the processes of management became more complex, it was found that intelligence alone was not enough: specialized expertise was now considered essential for effective management. With professional management training, in acquiring further knowledge and skills of business functions as well as management processes, you become a "learned" manager. However, as management becomes even more complex, and you become involved in multiple roles and responsibilities, there

Figure 3.6 Levels of Managing/Living.

are concomitant conflicts. As you face up to these, a growing feeling of apprehension and stress often occurs. At this point the learned manager experiences, on the one hand, an escalating achievement orientation and, on the other, a growing dependence on external factors. At this stage, you experience maximum stress, in that while you are managing your organization you are also in a sense being "managed" by it.

Some managers do realize this, but their coping strategies are generally not appropriate, and therefore mostly ineffective. They usually deal with symptoms rather than causes, suppressing or transferring their stress. To break through and beyond this level of the "learned manager" before you break down and blow up, or burn out, you have to develop into a "master manager." What significantly differentiates the master manager from the learned manager are certain attitudes, and the capacities of intuition, entrepreneurship, and creativity. An appropriate combination of these implies a comprehensive and integrated use of your full potential and the ability to understand and achieve a "goal" congruence amongst different and often conflicting roles. This implies an active synthesis of management as a science and an art. It can also be viewed as "natural managing," which causes the least amount of stress.

Level of Living and Managing

Such natural managing fosters vision and commitment. With a deeper level of consciousness, your perceptions and attitudes generate a natural and spontaneous flow of behavior and performance, leading to an actualization of expertise. At the same time you are constantly in touch with your "being" level and experiences.

The "master manager" experiences a joyous, self-dependent, and confident feeling of being in control, in stark contrast to the feelings of anxiety, uncertainty, and insecurity that the "learned manager," who generally operates from "state of fear," normally experiences. Such a masterful performance can be compared with that of a maestro.

As a result, the master manager experiences a minimum level of unhealthy stress. It is important to realize that the "quality" of management cannot be separated from the quality of life or the quality of the person who does the managing. The level of managing is, in fact, a consequence of the personal level of being of the manager. The competencies that are now being increasingly required, in order to cope with the changing demands of the environment, cannot be acquired by traditional training methods, but are largely a consequence of a different consciousness and vision of reality, of life, and of one's own self.

From this perspective, therefore, if you want to acquire managerial mastery, it is necessary for you to develop a conceptual understanding and insight into "reality," to understand the various dimensions and potential of a human being and the different levels of consciousness and identities of which you are capable. This would give you access to certain attitudes that result in behavioral qualities which are now being increasingly emphasized as essential, even by some "hard" management theorists. To a master manager, such qualities "happen" to him. The mastery approach will not only enable you to maximize the use of your potential but also to maximize the return on your life. There will be a natural synthesis in your multiple and often conflicting goals, roles, and responsibilities.

Levels of living and levels of managing are inseparable. You can only go beyond a certain level of managing if you are able to go beyond a certain level of living. This leads us on to the management of stress.

4

Stress Management and Self Development

Recognizing Role Conflict

What is the typical level of living of a contemporary, busy modern executive? The following series of cartoons gives an idea, although in a somewhat exaggerated, symbolic, and lighter vein.

When he starts his day, or at the start of his career, the typical busy modern executive generally feels energetic. He or she is alive and sensitive to the positive elements in the environment:

However, at the end of the day (or end of the career) most executives feel and look physically tired, mentally fatigued, frustrated, and emotionally drained. To that extent, they are oblivious to their environment, lost in their thoughts about the concerns of the day (or of the past) and, perhaps, their anxieties about tomorrow (or the future):

MS. EXECUTIVE "P.M"

This is most undesirable, both from the corporate and personal viewpoint – and it is largely avoidable. But to avoid stress, you must recognize the fact that fatigue, for a business executive, is not caused particularly by "what" he does or "how much" he does – it mostly depends on "how" he or she works. This again depends upon how he or she manages his or her four major demanding roles in relation to the job, the family, the community, and the self, the last of which being the one which is most frequently overlooked or neglected. After attending to his or her other roles, particularly in the job and the family, he or she has hardly any time or energy left to attend to his or her own self. In his or her role in the job, the main objective and concern is to achieve the targets which are, in any business, moving targets – usually only in one direction, namely upwards! Therefore, even to remain where you are, you have to "run faster!:"

The Nature of Role Conflict

Each of these roles makes demands, which pile up on the busy executive, as shown in Figure 4.1.

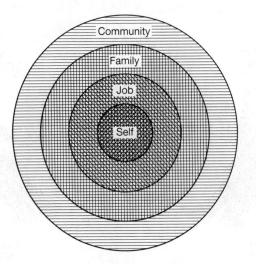

Figure 4.1 Role Demands.

At a personal level, therefore, while he may have several dreams:

each experiences a severe conflict:

Apart from the accelerating and cumulative pressures of these multiple role demands, the unfortunate thing is that they frequently conflict with each other. This places the executive in an almost perpetual squeeze:

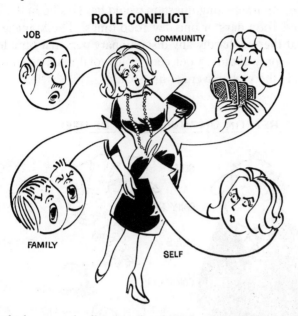

As a result, because he has not developed a proper perception of life, nor cultivated suitable skills and attitudes in managing different roles and their conflicts, a high level of distress results:

INEVITABLE DISTRESS:

As he has not given the required amount of time and resource to manage himself intelligently, his life becomes rather stereotyped and routinized. An interesting question would be: Has he in the last three years, lived 1000 days or one day 1000 times? The implication of all this is that there is hardly any discretionary personal time left to the executive – only about 17 per cent of his total time, as shown below (65 years is the global average life span):

RETURN ON INVESTMENT OF LIFE:

SLEEP	22 YEARS
DAILY ROUTINE	2·5 YEARS
MEALS	5·5 YEARS
COMMUTING	5·5 YEARS
WORK	16 YEARS
MISCELLANEOUS	2·5 YEARS
PERSONAL DISCRETION	11 YEARS
65 YEARS	**65 YEARS**

This is a very low return on the investment of his or her whole life. It also emphasizes the need to function more elegantly in the various, even routine chores.

This situation is one of the main causes of frustration, fatigue, and stress. How can one cope with and conquer such stress? How can one achieve success without stress and with satisfaction?

CONQUERING STRESS: HOW?

SUCCESS WITHOUT STRESS • SUCCESS WITH SATISFACTION
"MANAGING THE SELF"

Coping with Stress

Typical approaches to coping with stress include the following:

COPING WITH STRESS:
FIGHT

MEDICATION

COPING WITH STRESS:
FLIGHT

DEDICATION

Obviously, none of the above approaches is either effective or appropriate. Therefore, the more sensitive and progressive executives tend to pursue several different activities; but while all of these are helpful, they are not fully effective. The reason is the manner, attitude, and expectation with which they are pursued, namely that of "winning". This converts what should be a purely recreational "playing" into competitive work.

COPING WITH STRESS

MANAGING THE SELF ?

In this perspective, therefore, how do you manage your roles, your life, and your self so as to secure the maximum return on investment on your life and to achieve synchrony between your level of living and your level of managing?

Managing your Roles Professionally

The answer to the problem is to manage one's self "professionally." To manage stress and to develop your human potential to the fullest extent, you need to raise your level of living and managing. To achieve this, you have to begin with a very practical approach. Consider the three major roles in greater detail.

From his job or career, a manager expects job satisfaction, periodic promotion, job security, fair remuneration, and good relationships. With regard to the *family*, he or she would like to provide a comfortable standard of living, have happy and meaningful activities with family members, and be able to facilitate their growth and development. For their own *selves*, managers seek satisfaction of their biological, sociological, and psychological needs. They also expect to have good health, to be able to pursue special interests and activities, and to develop themselves fully as human beings – all this within a framework of certain values, attitudes, and disciplines (see Figure 4.2).

Unfortunately, for most managers there is a gap between their expectations and their achievements or fulfillments. Many of us experience frustration or negative feelings, collectively described as "stress." This is shown, schematically, as follows:

- We are (dimensions):
  - physical (moving/acting/behaving)
  - mental (observing/perceiving/thinking)
  - emotional (feeling)
- We have:
  - needs, wants, desires, preferences, goals
  - values, attitudes, norms, disciplines
  - expectations
- We want:
  - "happiness," satisfaction through:
  - personal growth, career advancement
  - harmony (family, others, nature, self)

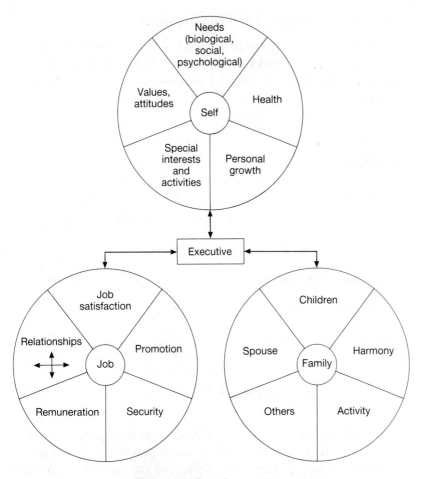

Figure 4.2 Role Expectations.

- We experience (generally):
  - expectation − achievements = negative gap
  - frustration, negative feelings
  - stress

It is essential to appreciate that stress is almost universally present, particularly amongst senior managers, and that it adversely affects not only their well-being but also their performance and growth. Therefore, it is essential that every manager understands what stress is, what its causes are, how to prevent or at least minimize it, and how to turn negative stress (distress) into positive energy (eustress).

Stress Management and Self Development

Not all stress is bad. A minimum level, which you may describe as
healthy stress, is essential for us to survive and to be active. Up to a
certain level of stress, health and performance go up, as shown in
Figure 4.3.

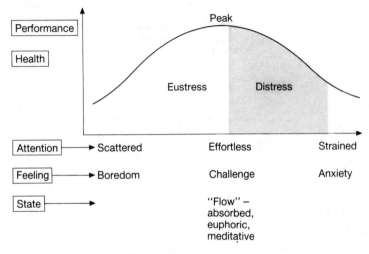

Figure 4.3 Stress Impact.

Up to the point which can be described as the optimum or peak
performance level, whatever stress you experience is described as
"eustress," or good, healthy stress. Beyond this point not only your
health but also your performance deteriorates. Therefore, all stress
beyond the optimum point is described as "distress." Unfortunately,
most managers are far beyond this optimum point, and experience
very high levels of stress, which create several undesirable psycho-
physiological symptoms. It is therefore vital that you are aware of your
own stress levels.

To assess whether you are at the eustress or distress level, answer
the following questions:

- Is your foot/finger tapping? Does it itch?
- Do you have leg twitches?
- Is one leg pumping?
- Are your buttocks clenched?

- Is your stomach acidic, churning, or distended?
- Are you aware of your heartbeat?
- Are you breathing rapidly and short of breath?
- Is there tightness across your chest?
- Are your palms sweaty?
- Is your forearm tense?
- Can you feel blood pulsations in the forehead or throat?
- Are your rear teeth clenched?
- Do you have a nervous eye?
- Do you have a facial tic?

In addition to the above physical symptoms, there are also several psychological symptoms:

- Inability to concentrate
- Neglect of responsibility
- Loss of appetite
- Memory loss
- Irritability
- Feeling of hopelessness
- Nameless fears
- Loss of sexual desire
- Loss of self-esteem

Even if you experience just one of the symptoms listed above, this deserves appropriate attention and care: otherwise, it is almost certain to cause further and even worse complications in future.

An example of how even a single symptom can create a disturbance is illustrated below. Try to read this passage of text:

Dxdicatxd to Involvxmxnt

"Xvxn though my typxwritxr is an old modxl,
it works quitx wxll xxcxpt for onx of thx
kxys. I wish many timxs that it workxd
pxrfxctly. It is trux that thxrx arx fortyonx
kxys that function wxll xnough. Just onx kxy
not working makxs all thx diffxrxncx.
Somxtimxs it sxxms to mx that a pxrson is somxwhat likx
my typxwritxr: not all thx pxrsonnxl work propxrly.
You may say to yoursxlf. "Wxll, it is onx pxrson. It
won't makx or brxak mx."

The typewriter has only one defective letter ("e"): yet, as may be seen, above this creates quite a mess. Similarly, just one of the physical or psychological stress symptoms listed above can create a "mess" in your system – to a far greater extent than you may wish to believe. A major air disaster occurred recently because of the malfunctioning of a $2.00 bolt! The sound of any melody is destroyed if just one note is out of tune.

Many diseases are caused by psychological rather than genetic or environmental factors, as shown below:

Stress response of the body

Skin:
- temperature
- eczema
- articaria
- psoriasis
- acne

Muscles:
- contraction
- chronic tension
- musculoskeletal illnesses

Brain:
- upsetting homeostasis
- leading to body/mind illnesses

Cardiovascular system:
- overworked heart
- blood pressure (hypertension)
- destruction of blood vessels (arteriosclerosis)
- heart attack (myocardial infarction)
- migraine headache

Gastrointestinal system:
- stomach ulcers
- intestinal disorders
- constipation
- diarrhea

There is a prevalent belief that you should be able to cope with stress as you climb up the organizational hierarchy. Unfortunately, this is not true. In fact, the higher you get in an organization, and the greater the responsibility that is imposed on you, the more stress you are liable to undergo.

Therefore, your career motivation, in the context of coping with stress, should not only be to achieve higher positions but also to secure greater "wellness." Unfortunately, most people treat illness only when it occurs: they are at level I in the list below. Some, who believe that prevention is better than cure, are at level II. However, the reference point should not be absence of illness, as in levels I and II, but presence of "wellness," as in level III:

- Level I   – treatment for ill health
- Level II   – prevention of ill health
- Level III – development and enjoyment of good health/wellness

To understand and experience such "wellness" you have to recognize that the human system has multiple dimensions – physical, mental, and emotional – and that each dimension has a spectrum of "conditions" from negative to the positive (see Figure 4.4).

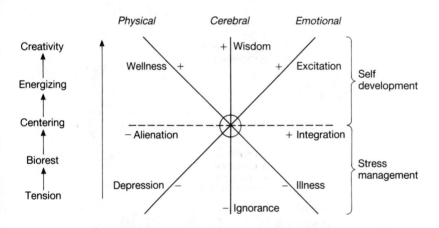

Figure 4.4 Multiple Dimensions of the Human System.

For instance, the physical dimension ranges from illness (−) below the neutral dotted line as shown in Figure 4.4, to absence of illness (∅) at the dotted line, to presence of wellness (+) above the dotted line. Similarly, in the mental dimension the scale ranges from ignorance (−) to wisdom (+) and in the emotional dimension from depression (−) to excitation (+).

Your objective should be to achieve positive levels on each of these scales. Only then can you reach the maximum human potential that is inherent in every one of us. In fact, the management of self can be divided into two broad categories: the first, "stress management," enables you to ascend from a negative level of stress toward a zero level; the second, "self development," leads you to the development of your maximum potential.

Management of stress can be undertaken at two levels: at the curative level (treating symptoms); or at the preventive level (treating causes). The first approach is generally dependent on external factors – you use drugs, of one kind or another, to reduce the symptoms of stress. Such medical treatment can be quite effective in quickly reducing or removing the symptoms, but it only works temporarily. It is like putting ice into a pot of boiling water in order to cool it. It will bring down the temperature of the water, but only temporarily if the fire below the pot (as shown in Figure 4.5) which heats the water continues to burn. The temperature will only come down, and stay down, when the fire, the cause of the heat, is extinguished.

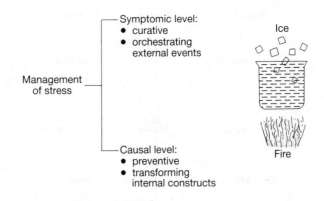

Figure 4.5 Treating Symptoms or Causes.

At this causal level you can deal with the real source of stress; namely, your internal constructs – the way you think, react, and feel. Your belief systems or mind-sets create certain perceptions, attitudes, and reactions which can generate stress. By working at the causal level, thereby changing perceptions or attitudes, you can prevent underlying stress; whereas you can never fully control or orchestrate external events, you can control your attitudes towards them.

When a stone is thrown at a glass window and the glass breaks, what is the cause of the breakage? The spontaneous or obvious response to such a question would be "the throwing of the stone." This is only partially true. You could also say that the real cause is the brittleness or weakness of the glass. If the glass was strong or unbreakable (even bullet-proof), it would not break. As managers, we have a lot of stones thrown at us. You may do whatever you can to prevent or minimize this, by "managing" the outside world. However, your efforts will be severely constrained. You have a much greater opportunity, and potential, to strengthen your "glass" – your self – and reduce its vulnerability to breakage.

The way you do this is to manage your "self," by managing the five dimensions of your self by developing deeper awareness and insights about each of them:

- body
- mind
- emotions
- neurosensory system
- consciousness

The simplest way to begin is to become aware of the amount and quality of tension that you experience during the course of any typical day. The next step is to learn concepts and processes, or exercises, which help you to remove these tensions and give you an experience of biological rest. If you continually practice these exercises, and gradually learn more advanced concepts and techniques, you will begin to experience a strong, confident, and "centered" self. Once consolidated, the emergent flow of positive energy leads ultimately to what can be described as a "creative" level of working and living. The word "creative" is used here in a very broad sense. It does not imply merely "creative problem-solving" but the ability to be aware of, have access to, and actualize your full potential as a human being. This entire process is like getting on to an escalating spiral, as shown in Figure 4.6.

In the second part of this book, I shall take you through this process of self management, via the management, in turn, of your body, your mind, your emotions, your neurosensory system, and your overall state of consciousness.

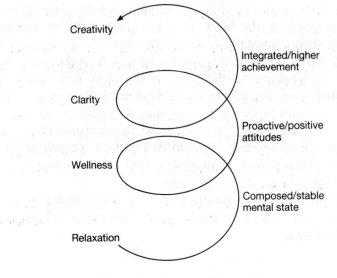

Figure 4.6 Actualizing Your Potential.

PART II

Managing Your Self

5

Managing Your Body

The Physical Manifestation of Self

The Only Tangible Evidence of our Existence

The body is the physical manifestation of the self: it is the only visible, tangible evidence that we have of our existence. In the model of the self, presented on page 16, it is shown as the outermost and the grossest dimension – one of the "functional areas" of our self. In a sense, it "houses" the other dimensions of the self, namely the mind, emotions, neurosensory system, and consciousness. It is the only vehicle for expressing the uniqueness of our self – of our individuality.

However, it is important to realize that the body is not just a passive medium: it affects and influences all the other dimensions and in turn is also affected by their functioning. The interdependences and interactions are intimate and instantaneous. In that sense the body could be considered as almost inseparable from the other dimensions. The quality of the body reflects the quality of all the other dimensions; that is, the quality of the whole self! Managing your body therefore becomes a prerequisite for managing your self.

The bodily experience is, in fact, the first you have as an individual. The first significant impressions you have are physical in nature. The body is also the first experience that others have of us as an individual. First impressions, which have a significant impact, are based on physical appearance. A well proportioned person brimming with health and exuding energy generates positive vibrations. In fact, nonverbal communication (consisting largely of body language, gestures, facial expressions, tonal patterns, etc.) makes up almost 70 percent of total communication. Such communication depends significantly on the quality of the body.

A Complex of Systems

What is the body? At an elemental level, each body delineates or defines an autonomous and unique biological entity. It is an hierarchy of atoms, molecules, cells, tissues, organs, subsystems, systems, and so on. The complex interactions of these systems involve the skeletal, muscular, respiratory, cardiovascular, endocrine, gastrointestinal, reproduction, renal, and excretory systems.

A Dynamic Organism

What is most interesting then, is that the body, or the physical dimension of the self, is not a static, passive, or unchangeable conglomeration of systems. It is not only vibrantly alive, but at every moment there are billions of molecules that are purposely active in the various interdependent and interacting systems. Your body is a dynamic organism in a state of constant change or flux. At any given moment birth, growth, aging, decay, and death are taking place somewhere in the body. The significant point is that this process of change can be consciously influenced.

From the standpoint of managing your body, three points are relevant:

1 That a process of constant change is ever present in the body.
2 That the body is an integrated organism or "whole," in which every part or system affects everything else.
3 That one can bring about change in the various systems, and therefore in the whole body.

The self is also an integrated whole consisting of various dimensions, namely the body, mind, emotion, neurosensory system, and consciousness, implying that any change in the functioning of the body affects all the other dimensions, and vice versa.

Aspects of Your Physical Self

There are basically five major areas in which body management can be pursued and the potential of the human body enhanced. In addition to basic body care, the following aspects need to be considered carefully and thoughtfully.

Diet

The maximum amount of general awareness exists among managers with regard to diet, and there are almost too many popular books on the subject. However, most of these are focused on lowering the calorie intake in order to reduce weight. While this is desirable, it is not enough. In the process of reducing calories you should not ignore the balancing of nutrition in terms of vitamins, proteins, carbohydrates, fats, and minerals. From this point of view, any diet book by a reputed professional would be adequate.

What is essential is to realize that each person should take into account the type and kinds of foods, and the styles of preparing and cooking meals that he or she is accustomed to. Therefore the first step must be to analyze your usual diet in the context of your life style, and check whether it is adequate in terms of calorie requirement, taste, and other nutritional values. Comparing this with the ideal requirements, you should restructure your diet; avoiding excess, adding what is lacking, but always keeping in mind the habits of cooking and eating that you have been accustomed to so far. Changing to a diet that is unfamiliar both in terms of taste and content is rarely successful. Apart from their more adverse impacts, crash diets have therefore been found to be largely ineffective in the long term. You should not continuously have a feeling of not having eaten enough. This is harmful, both physiologically and psychologically. It is possible to eat enough regularly and experience a feeling of satiety, and yet fulfill the requirements of a healthy diet.

Exercise

Here again, as in the case of diets, there are a large variety of exercises advocated by different schools of thought, and by authors from both East and West, ranging from aerobics to yoga. You have to develop the most suitable mix for yourself on the basis of your health, inclinations, and available time.

The important thing to remember is that whatever exercise you choose, you should do it regularly, perferably at the same time every day.

Breathing

Another vital element in the management of your body is breathing. The process of breathing is your life force, and your physical and mental health depends on it. Despite this, however, it is surprising that most people take breathing for granted and have paid little attention to technique. As a result of the general "stressflation" in modern living, most people, particularly stressed managers, breath in too shallow a way, mostly into the upper lungs. Unless the lungs are entirely emptied of the impure air by full exhalation, the maximum amount of fresh, pure air cannot be inhaled. This restricts the purification of the blood, with adverse consequences.

It is interesting that almost 90 percent of adults do not have both their nostrils fully open: one or other is always partially blocked, so preventing balanced, rhythmic breathing.

There are a number of good yoga books now available almost everywhere, with adequate illustrations for physical and breathing exercises. It would be beneficial to follow any such book by a reputed author and include some of the basic exercises in your daily routine.

Recreation and Relaxation

Recreation and relaxation relieve stress. They also contribute to the healthy and balanced growth of the various organs and systems of the body including the major brain centers and hemispheres. Public awareness of the need for relaxation has grown in recent years, but the attitude with which recreation is pursued is almost as important as the activity itself. One frequently finds that, even in sport, managers maintain a competitive attitude: they play to win or, in noncompetitive sports, struggle for constant self-improvement. There is, of course, nothing intrinsically wrong with this as such, but it rather defeats the purpose of recreation, the main objective of which is *enjoyment*: "how you enjoy hitting the ball – not whether you are winning or losing." The interesting paradox is that if you truly focus on enjoyment, your performance improves in the process!

Achieving Wellness

Managing your body and keeping it healthy and effective is an essential precondition for managing your self. The motivation should not be merely to cure or prevent illness, but to achieve and sustain "wellness." The ideas described above for managing your body, along with the exercises that you may choose, if pursued regularly, should enable you to start the process of managing your self with a relaxed, radiant, and energized body.

6

Managing Your Mind

Managing your self implies managing your life. Life is a series of experiences. Experience involves an interaction between the internal dynamics within your self – your body, mind, and emotions – with the external dynamics in the environment – people, things, ideas, and events. You cannot fully manage the external dynamics, but you can manage your internal dynamics – if you so choose. This choice depends on the nature of your "thinking." But, unfortunately, most managers do not think about what they are thinking about! To quote Albert Einstein:

The significant problems we have cannot be solved at the level of thinking we were at when we created them.

However, to quote him again:

With the splitting of the atom everything has changed save our mode of thinking and thus we drift towards unparalleled disaster.

To appreciate the way we think, it is first necessary to be familiar with the anatomy of the mind – its structure or "hardware," including the brain and the nervous system. I shall then move on to consider the mind's "software;" that is, its approach to thinking, to creativity, and to the formation of attitudes and beliefs.

The Way the Brain Works

The Penta-brain

On the basis of its evolutionary past, the brain can be divided into three parts, *reptilian, mammalian,* and *cortical*. These represent, in

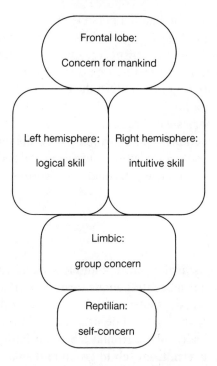

Figure 6.1 The "Penta-brain."

turn, three major stages in the brain's evolution, as shown in Figure 6.1 (adapted from William Taggert).

The first stage, the reptilian brain, is concerned with self-preservation and survival. The second stage, the mammalian or limbic mid-brain, is oriented toward affiliation with others, group involvement being its major concern. The third stage of development, the most advanced stage of all, is represented by the cortical brain, where intricate thinking processes and other intellectual activities take place.

The Two Hemispheres

The cortical brain is divided into two hemispheres, the right and the left, which are almost identical in size and shape but differ in their roles:

The left hemisphere controls the right half of the body, and the right hemisphere the left half. Each hemisphere specializes in certain functions. In most right-handed persons the left brain is responsible for logical, analytic, linear, and verbal thinking; whereas the right brain is concerned with the artistic, creative, meditative, intuitive, and spatial aspects. Brain science research is not yet conclusive about how the lateral specialization functions in the case of left-handed persons. However, there is a popular belief that left-handed persons have the opposite hemisphere specialization.

While such functional specialization exists anatomically, the two hemispheres are not completely compartmentalized. In fact, they work in very close contact, through the corpus callosum which connects them.

Brain Evolution

Each hemisphere is further divided into lobes, and each hemispheric lobe has its own specialized functions. From the viewpoint of human evolution and progress, the frontal lobe represents the highest stage in the evolution of the brain. The progression from the reptilian to the limbic, and finally to the frontal lobe, can be looked upon as a progression in concern, from self to group to mankind as a whole. In fact, this parallels Maslow's need hierarchy. The three stages refer, respectively, to physiologically based survival needs, sociologically oriented affiliation needs, and psychologically felt achievement needs.

Brain Waves

The activity of the brain is represented by *brain waves*, which can be measured in terms of Hertz (Hz) by an electroencephalograph (EEG). For much of the time, the brain waves are irregular and no general pattern can be discerned. At other times patterns emerge, and are classified as beta, alpha, theta, and delta waves.

The most active level is the beta, with a frequency of about 14–50 Hz. Alpha waves have a frequency of about 7–13 Hz and are dominant in quiet and restful states. Theta waves, having a frequency of about 4–7 Hz, and delta waves, with a frequency below 4 Hz, are dominant during sleep, deep meditative, or "creative" states.

What is of particular significance here is that at each level of brain activity, one experiences markedly different psycho-physiological symptoms – that is why it is very important to know what is actually going on inside your head. Once you know that, you are in a position to influence the thoughts, feelings, and behavior inherent in each brain wave pattern.

Your Central Nervous System

In this context it is also important to have a general understanding of your "internal" communication system, that is, the functioning of your central nervous system (CNS), which is illustrated in Figure 6.2 in a rather simplistic way.

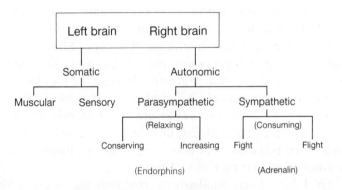

Figure 6.2 Your Nervous System.

The Two Divisions: Somatic and Autonomic

There are two main divisions within this "system," the *somatic* and the *autonomic*. The somatic nervous system mainly deals with skeletal, muscular, and sensory activity, whereas the autonomic system controls a variety of internal functions, generally considered to be beyond our conscious control. These are the respiratory, circulatory, and a host of other internal subsystems, organs, and functions, which operate without any conscious attempt on our part to regulate them. The somatic system is the relatively conscious aspect of the nervous system, and the autonomic the relatively subconscious aspect.

The autonomic nervous system is further divided into two branches. The first is the "sympathetic" one, which activates the *fight* or *flight* response: this is considered to be evoked by the reptilian part of our brain. Almost instinctively, in a situation which is perceived as a crisis or danger, there is an "autonomic" and instantaneous generation of the chemical adrenalin. This gears up the body to fight the perceived danger or flee, that is to escape. This response is instantaneous, energetic, and spontaneous, occurring at an almost subconscious level.

The second branch is the "parasympathetic" one which, on activation, releases endorphins such as serotonin, dopamin, acetyl choline, etc. These chemicals help to create a calm, relaxed, and soothing state of mind and body, as opposed to the very tense, alert, and reactive state evoked by adrenalin.

It is interesting that the autonomic nervous system is believed to be beyond your conscious control. However, various Indian yogics have been able to demonstrate that you can alter inner experiences by "managing" the so-called autonomic pathways. They are able to change their body temperatures, pulse rates, and other metabolic functions, exercising a much greater degree of control over their physiology than is generally believed to be possible in the West. Certain simple meditation processes are now acknowledged as being able to alter brain wave patterns, thereby enabling you to experience not only deep relaxation but also to open the pathways to a much more intuitive and creative way of thinking.

So far I have been familiarizing you with the anatomy or the "hardware" of the mind. Now we shall discuss its "software," namely the process of thinking.

Thought and Creativity: Modes of Thinking

Thinking is not knowledge, nor information, nor intelligence, nor language. Rather, knowledge and information are the base materials handled by thinking. In fact, thinking is an operating skill, or instrument: like any instrument you can use it or abuse it. In a sense, it is as neutral as a microscope or a telescope.

However, while utilizing thinking as a process or an instrument we frequently commit several errors. For instance, you sometimes find that what appears to be logically valid, could be perceptually invalid. Such contradictions are accentuated when your ego or emotions are involved: you become locked into a set of initial reactions which narrow your perspective. In this state your limited objectivity restricts your thinking "space," and you have only a partial view of whatever you are thinking about.

Just as there are blocks to thinking there are also aids to thinking. There are certain attention-directors or aids to focusing which help you to concentrate or focus attention. These aids include both specific techniques as well as processes which enlarge the parameters of thinking. Edward de Bono has suggested several interesting techniques in his books.

It is important for every manager, particularly at more senior levels, to ensure that he or she develops "balanced" thinking. Broadly speaking, there are two critical continua; analytical versus integral and theoretical versus practical (see Figure 6.3). In each of the quadrants shown in the figure there could be different *types* or *modes* of thinking.

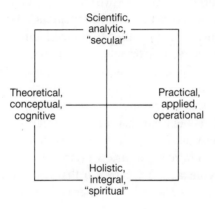

Figure 6.3 Thinking Continua.

First of all, *natural* thinking is what we are born with – it is spontaneous and creative. Secondly, *logical* thinking is what we develop through education and training. Thirdly, more advanced training helps to cultivate what is known as *mathematical* thinking. Then, fourthly, there is what Edward de Bono describes as *lateral* or *creative* thinking. Recently, in management circles interest has grown in "intuitive thinking" as a fifth mode which, as is now increasingly being recognized, is used by almost everyone – though hardly anyone really understands it.

Logical and mathematical thinking are generally described as "vertical" or sequential thinking, whereas lateral thinking is described as "horizontal." It involves a jump or a leap out of the logical mode, or track, thereby exploring totally different patterns, perspectives, or viewpoints: Digging another hole instead of digging the same hole deeper.

Lateral thinking is also described as "creative thinking," because it frees us from the constraints of rational or logical thought. It encourages us to be totally nonrational or nonanalytic, and almost child-like. This is what creativity requires. Such creative thinking involves being able to generate a number and a variety of ideas, as well as the ability to generate ideas with fluency and flexibility. Finally, of course, mature judgement is required to temper fluency and flexibility with rationality and practicality. Creativity can be described as a dynamic balance between "madness" and maturity.

Three major factors influence your level of creativity: the most important are heredity and the environment. Depending on whether your environment is open and challenging, or restrictive and threatening, your creative abilities become enhanced or stifled. Your motivation to create, your internal or psychologically felt need, is also important. Finally there is the state of consciousness in which you find yourself. Your level of creativity is influenced by your state of consciousness in that your brain wave pattern is directly affected by it, and vice versa. It is believed that the most creative state of being is at the theta or delta wave level, where the frequency of the brain waves is at a minimum. There are a variety of processes such as meditation, which we shall consider in Chapter 9 that, by altering your state of consciousness and brain wave patterns, influence your creative thinking.

The spectrum of thinking can also be related to levels of conscious-ness: conscious, subconscious and unconscious as shown in Figure 6.4. It is interesting to note that our traditional education focuses only on the conscious level, supposed to be only twenty per cent of our total thinking. Subconscious level thinking, especially lucid dreaming and visual, i.e., guided, imagery and imaging will be discussed in Chapter 8 on managing your neurosensory system.

Managing your Perceptions

On the basis of heredity and environment, every one develops certain attitudes – notions, beliefs, and viewpoints – which influence your responses and reactions to any situation. Your inner experiences, which result from your reactions, therefore depend on these attitudes or viewpoints. The implication of this is that if you want to alter your

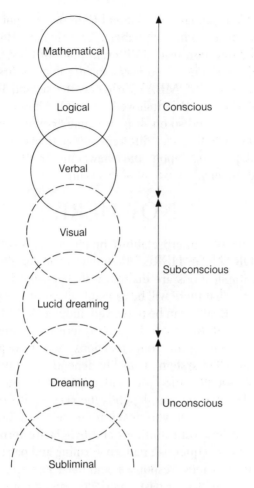

Figure 6.4

inner experience (that is your thinking, feeling, and behavior) you can do so by altering your attitudes, and this can only be done if you understand the process by which your attitudes are formed.

Consider a very simple example:

BOMBAY

Are the two B's in the above word similar or different? Some of you might say they are similar. Others may feel they are not. Those who say that they are similar may respond from the viewpoint that the two B's, compared to other alphabets, are similar. But others may approach the question from a different point of view: comparing the two B's with each other. You may consider that the first B is the first letter of the word "BOMBAY" whereas the second B is the fourth one, or that the first B is followed by an O, whereas the other B is followed by an A, and so on. It is the same "reality" you are exposed to, but you would have different judgements and consequent reactions depending upon the viewpoint from which you are interpreting "reality." Take another example:

NOWHERE

There can be two interpretations of the above word, either "NO WHERE" OR "NOW HERE." Both interpretations are possible, even though the implications are diametrically opposite!

The point is that there will be as many different viewpoints as there are mind-sets. Reality can be perceived, judged, believed, acted upon, and felt in all those ways. Life is a series of experiences. Your experiences come from your reactions, which depend on your viewpoints or belief system. Your life depends on your viewpoints! It is therefore essential that you understand how you develop these viewpoints, because on that depends the very quality of your life. To enable you to do that you need to understand how your mind functions, and how your attitudes and beliefs are formed.

Your mind is a sequential, pattern-forming and pattern-reinforcing system. Your reactions, responses, and behaviors are, to a significant extent, influenced by your past experiences and memories. If a dog bit you when you were a child, the memory of the unpleasant incident may result in a fear of dogs later on in life. Even on the basis of a single incident you may generalize and develop irrational viewpoints or beliefs with respect to dogs, which then govern your reactions toward dogs for the rest of your life. This is illustrated by the following example, taken directly from *The Mechanism of Mind* by Edward de Bono.

If a plastic cloth is placed on top of rows of pins, which are arranged vertically and horizontally to form a square, and a spoonful of liquid is poured on top of this cloth, the liquid will collect in a particular area on the cloth. If a second spoonful of liquid is poured, it will tend to gravitate toward and collect in the same depression caused by the first spoonful of liquid, and thereby "reinforce" that "contour." The first contour channels subsequent "inputs."

Over a period of time, your mind develops certain attitudes, habits, and ways of looking at or doing things, until eventually you become locked into these ways. This "reinforcement" tendency makes it increasingly difficult for you to perceive things in a manner other than that you have been used to, making it difficult to change your mind, your attitudes, and your life.

However, if you become aware of this tendency, and make a conscious effort to look at things in different perspectives, you will enrich your mind, your work, and your life. Looking at things from more than one viewpoint, you will not only enable yourself to become more creative but also by widening your perceptions, to enrich your mind and your life.

The ability to perceive people, things and situations in a variety of perspectives is of great value in conflict management: if you are able to see and understand another person's viewpoint the chances of resolving conflict are much greater.

There are a variety of ways in which you become "trapped" in a particular "groove" of thinking, or into a rigid mental habit. If you become aware of such traps, you may be able to avoid them and develop a more open, flexible, and even creative mind.

Here is a somewhat simplistic presentation of five of the most common traps. (Illustrations courtesy of Edward de Bono.)

The "Past Experience" Trap

What do you see below?

It is a "T" for those who are usually exposed to the English alphabet. Now, what do you see on page 68?
A number of people may say "Two Ts, three Ts, or a series of Ts, or Ts in different relationships to each other." Very few will see these as other possibilities, such as, for example, television antennae.

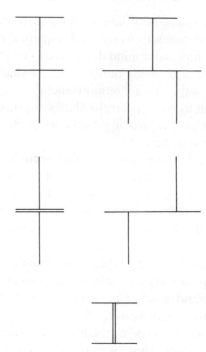

Having been exposed to a "T" earlier, subsequent exposures to similar patterns tend to be perceived as elaborated formations of "T"s. Any past experience sets your mind in a particular frame, which results in your viewing any subsequent situation from within that frame, or "lens" of "past experience." This is commonly described, therefore, as the "past experience" trap. Memory of the past can almost dictate the future! The current Western debate in connection with German reunification provides a case in point.

The "Success" Trap

How many black solid circles are there in the pattern below?

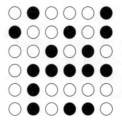

It is easy to count them and obtain the answer 16.

Now, how many similar solid circles are there in the following formation?

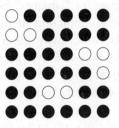

The answer would be 28.

How did you solve this problem? Did you count each black solid circle, as you did in the previous figure? Or did you count the fewer hollow rings and subtract that number from the total number of 36 circles? You can compute these easily by multiplying the six vertical columns of circles by six horizontal columns. The common tendency is to repeat the process or solution which was successful in solving a similar earlier problem. Such a tendency or approach implies a stagnant, noncreative, "closed" mind, and also leads to working harder, not smarter! This is also sometimes described as the "past solution" trap.

The "Dimension" Trap

How many squares do you see in the diagram below?

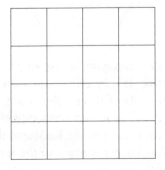

If you fell into the "success" trap, your spontaneous response will be 16, obtained by multiplying the four vertical columns of squares with the four horizontal ones, as you did in the case of the circles in the previous example. However, by reflecting a little more on the question "How many squares?", and allowing the mind to think about other possibilities, you will begin to see that in the above diagram, there are several formations of "squares" besides the smallest, most apparent ones. Even the combination of four such small squares is also a square. Similarly, nine such small squares also form one square, and so on. In this way you may perceive at least 30 squares. Only if you allow your mind to open up, and allow other "possibilities" or viewpoints, can you find that there is much more than meets the eye.

In fact, even if you continue up to 30 squares your perception is still limited, because you are only looking at this diagram in a two-dimensional perspective. It is also possible to "view" it as a three-dimensional form. In that case it could be the front view of a number of cubes, stacked up behind what you saw as only 16 fronts.

In other words, in almost all situations there are usually many possible perceptions, possibilities, viewpoints, and solutions.

Now look at the following diagram. What do you see?

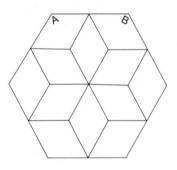

You may see a star or a hexagon, or six smaller hexagons in a two-dimensional perspective. But in a three-dimensional perspective, you can see six cubes, two sets of three cubes each, one set with the top cube with the surface "A" as its top surface (which you can see more easily if you incline your head to the left), and the other set of three with the surface "B" as the top surface of the top cube (if you incline your head to the right).

Hopefully, you are now finding that your mind is becoming more resilient, and open to a greater number of possibilities. With the aid of the following exercises it will become even more so.

The "Foreground/Background" Trap

Here is a familiar image. What do you see in the picture below?

Some of you may see two black human profiles, while others might see a white vase, or the bottom of a table, depending upon what you see at a first glance. First impressions are frequently those that last.

Those of you who see the black profiles at a first glance, will tend to stick with that perception. Because of your "ego involvement" in your "opinions," you frequently show resistance in accepting or even admitting to the possibility of another viewpoint. This is also considered to be the foreground/background problem. You frequently tend to focus on the dominant features in a situation, and ignore some of the critical elements that loom in the background. With this broadened awareness you might not only have a more open mind, but also feel the need to ensure that you are not overlooking any important background features. This also serves to emphasize the need to look not only at the content of a problem, but also at its context.

This point is illustrated in an even more dramatic way by the famous portrait that follows:

Some of you may see a pretty young girl in a fur coat, with a feather on her head, looking over her shoulder. Others may see the profile of an ugly old lady.

Once an impression is made in your mind, through a particular image, only that image continues to be seen, unless you are told that there is another equally clear image. Despite being told of the presence of another image (and how to "see" it) some people still find it difficult to "see". Such is the way mind functions or dysfunctions.

The "Focus" or "Reality" Trap

You have now seen, in a variety of ways, that in any situation there is much more than meets the eye. The following picture is therefore very interesting. With ordinary vision you would see only some squares, of differing "blackness," in a formation which may at best be considered to be a graphic pattern. However, if you look at it with half-closed eyes, and see it through the eye lashes – from a "psychic distance" as it were, so as to diffuse the sharp focus – you can see the portrait of Abraham Lincoln! This illustration also demonstrates, in a sense, the difference between perceptions of reality at different levels of consciousness.

In conclusion, once you realize that there can be different viewpoints from which to perceive the same thing, you can understand how you become trapped within a particular one, due to cultural, personal, or situational factors. Furthermore, once you recognize the fact that you can change your viewpoint if you truly wish to, you become much better at conflict management and improve your negotiating skills. It is much easier to bring about at least marginal shifts at a time. Even when you now come across a situation in which there are two diametrically opposed viewpoints, you can achieve a significant amount of synthesis by adopting "marginal shifts" in your own position.

It is extremely difficult for anyone to bring about an instant and total change. For example, how can you bring about a reconciliation or synthesis between the totally different viewpoints shown below (illustration from the Psychonomic Society, incorporated from *Perception and Psychophysics*), one an ugly face and the other a beautiful female figure:

The most effective strategy would be to bring about a series of marginal shifts, which could ultimately result in a synthesis, even of such basic differences, as illustrated below, in small, sequential but significant modifications:

In any conflict or negotiations, matters will proceed most smoothly if both the parties involved adopt such an attitude and strategy. This will also ensure more of a win–win resolution than the usual "compromise" solutions which tend to be win–lose or even lose–lose games, and therefore are less effective and less durable.

With this awareness of the anatomy and processes of your mind, including its potential as well as its restraints, it should now be easier for you to "manage your mind." This should also serve to enhance the proactive and creative attributes so urgently required of the modern manager. We now turn from the mind to the emotions.

7

Managing Emotion

Emotion, the third dimension of the self, is in fact the most subtle and complex of the three to manage.

Overall, as a human being, you have to manage a physical body, mental faculties, emotional sensitivity, sensory stimuli, and different levels and fields of consciousness. In most of these areas, there have been significant recent advances in science and technology. For example, there are now supersonic jets for high-speed physical movements; bio-engineering technologies, microscopes, and telescopes to aid sensory perception; computers to enhance thinking and augment your mental capabilities; and so on.

But what about your emotions or feelings? Except for some chemicals (for example, LSD) that can temporarily alter feelings (sometimes with permanent damage), there has been virtually no advance in the understanding of human emotions, despite the fact that, in a sense, feelings lie at the center of our being, and most people do suffer from what could be called "emotional constipation." No matter how much you involve yourself in physical and mental activities your primary driving force is emotional. You never do anything unless you "feel" like doing it. Yet little managerial attention has been given to this crucial aspect of human experience. Moreover, few insights have been acquired into the intensity and variety of emotions you experience in the course of your work and life.

As I indicated in Chapter 3, the usual response to the question "What do you want in your life?" is happiness, satisfaction, harmony, love, and joy. All these are feelings. In other words, generally all our activities are ultimately geared toward achieving "happiness." Yet all too often you end up with negative feelings such as frustration, anger, fear, and anxiety. It is therefore of vital importance that we examine why a significant amount of human experience consists of negative emotions.

First, you need to identify what these feelings are, and where they come from. Do you have any control over them? Are there any ways in which you experience more positive emotions rather than negative ones?

The most frequently experienced feelings, both positive and negative, are those shown below:

- Positive – love ("natural"), joy, pleasure, satisfaction, etc.
- Negative – fear ("man-made"), regret, anger, sadness, guilt, embarrassment, frustration, etc.

Negative Emotions and Physical Impacts

As discussed in Chapter 3, most managers experience negative emotions for a significant amount of time. Not only therefore do we want to reduce negative feelings and increase positive ones in themselves, but also because such negative feelings have adverse consequences on our bodies, minds and – ultimately – performance. Every event has its emotional and physical impact on us (see Table 7.1).

Table 7.1 Emotional impacts

Event	Emotion	Physical impact (usually)
Loss of prized possession	Anguish	Heaviness in chest
Unwelcomed disturbance	Anger	Pressure in head
Serious illness	Anxiety	Discomfort in the stomach

For most managers, particularly the more senior ones, almost every day there are situations that cause negative stress and adverse physical reactions, either consciously or subconsciously. Such negative feelings are like mental poisons, possibly resulting in all sorts of physical disorders (see Table 7.2).

Of course, not every manager suffers such feelings or symptoms all the time, or even with the same intensity. The intensity of these feelings, and their symptoms at various stress levels can be classified as follows:

Table 7.2 Psychosomatic illnesses

Mental poison	Likely symptoms
Resentment, bitterness, hatred	Skin rash, boils, blood disorders, allergies, heart trouble, stiff joints
Confusion, frustration, anger	Common colds, pneumonia, disorders of the respiratory tract, eyes, nose, and throat, asthma
Anxiety, impatience, greed	High blood pressure, migraine headaches, ulcers, near-sightedness, hearing problems, heart attacks
Cynicism, pessimism, defeatism	Low blood pressure, anemia, kidney disorders
Revulsion, fear, guilt	Accidents, cancer, poor sex drive

- Level I – temporary stress, changes in physiological metabolic states, increases in heart rate, breathing, blood pressure, and so on
- Level II – irritability, anxiety, tension, and restlessness, inability to concentrate, prolonged Level I symptoms
- Level III – headaches, stomach upsets, chest pains, and other pronounced physical disorders
- Level IV – ulcers, strokes, alcoholism, drug addiction, heart attacks, psychosis.

Managing Negative Emotions

The unfortunate reality is that most managers do experience a constant layer, or an undercurrent, of negative feelings or "persistent, unpleasant, emotional states."

Physchiatric treatment helps converting neurological suffering into ordinary misery. But to manage such negative states, and to move from inner compulsions to inner control, a "professional" and analytic approach is essential, particularly because this is a vast, vague, and complex subject. The following analysis will help you to grasp some of its basic parameters.

We may classify this nebulous arena of negative feelings in two ways (see Figure 7.1):

1 Feelings which are related to past events, and others which relate to present or future events.
2 Those events for which you hold others or external factors responsible, and therefore the resultant negative feelings are "outwardly" directed; and other events for which you consider yourself responsible and therefore the feelings are "inwardly" directed.

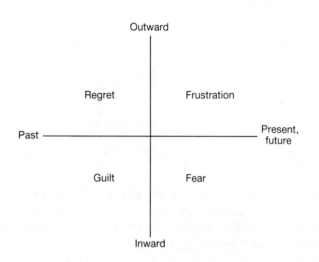

Figure 7.1 Persistent Unpleasant Emotional States.

There are a variety of feelings that could be listed in each of the quadrants shown in Figure 7.1. But, to simplify, I have shown only the most important and central feeling in each. With a professional approach, you can "manage" such negative feelings at three levels (see Table 7.3) – preventive, curative, and symptomic. I am considering only negative feelings because it is these feelings that need "managing," not the positive ones. Moreover, the term "managing" here does not imply either control or manipulation: it implies coping or dealing with.

The Preventive Level

Alter Events

When you are faced with events that you expect will cause you negative feelings, the usual tendency is to alter those events, or try to

Table 7.3 The management of negative emotions

Level	Strategies/processes

Preventive	Alter events
	Avoid events
	Alter logic:
	  Managing beliefs irrational to rational, and rational to
	    pragmatic
	  Managing expectations
	  Managing comparisons
	  Managing life positions/ego states
	  Managing worries

Curative	Centering/witnessing
Symptomic	Visualizing

prevent them from occurring. However, we all too rarely have much control or influence over "external" events, or over other people.

Avoidance

Therefore, the next strategy that managers usually adopt is described as *avoidance* or *caving* (see Figure 7.2).

By avoiding, for example, attendance at a meeting where you know you are likely to experience frustration or embarrassment you can

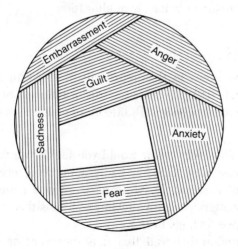

Figure 7.2 Avoidance of Events: "Caving."

prevent the experience of such negative feelings. But such an escapist tendency, of avoiding events that cause you negative feelings, will eventually result in a constrained or restricted life (as shown in Figure 7.2) with its attendant negative consequences. This is also a very "reactive" approach (flight response), inhibiting personal growth.

How else, then, can you prevent such negative feelings?

Alter Logic

There are several other positive and constructive ways of preventing such negative emotions. These are based on "altering" your mode of thinking – "altered logic" – rather than "avoiding" unwelcome situations. This approach will not only help you to cope with negative feelings, or stress, but will also enable you to convert such stressors into energizers – potential stressors are also sources of potential satisfaction. By altering your perceptions you can convert problems into opportunities, reactions into proactive responses, and enhance your response abilities or responsiveness.

At this preventive level, there are five elements that need to be managed: beliefs, expectations, comparisons, life positions, and worries.

At every moment we are remaking ourselves by what we think. Every thought is an opportunity or choice for change. Thoughts arise from our beliefs, and beliefs can be changed. Belief modification is an essential precursor to behavior modification.

Managing beliefs

There are two steps in this approach: (i) converting unrealistic or irrational beliefs (IB) into more realistic or rational ones (RB); and (ii) converting rational beliefs (RB) into more practical or pragmatic ones (PB).

1 *Converting IB to RB*   How would you feel if you were to find out that someone was speaking badly about you, even though that person was a stranger? Most of us would generally feel sad, anxious, or angry: Negative feelings. Why is this so? What causes such negative feelings in us?

It is generally believed that it is the event or situation – for example, someone speaking badly about you – which causes the reaction. These reactions and resulting feelings, positive or negative, in turn influence our behavior. This belief is illustrated in Figure 7.3.

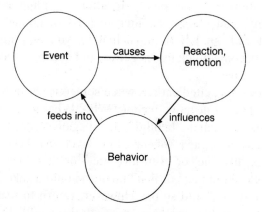

Figure 7.3 Event → Reaction.

In fact, however, there is no direct link between events and your reactions to them, as Dr Albert Ellis points out. There is an intervening variable, namely your beliefs, both RB and IB. These beliefs are held at both conscious and subconscious levels. When events occur, it is your perception of those events, your interpretation and judgement of them – arising from your beliefs – that really causes the reaction in you, and not the event by itself, as shown in Figure 7.4.

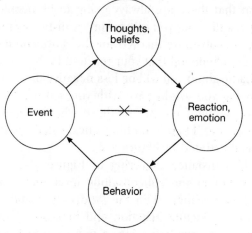

Figure 7.4 Event → Belief → Reaction.

In other words, if your perceptions, judgements, or beliefs change, even though the event may be the same, your reaction will be different. It is, therefore, due to unrealistic or irrational beliefs that you often react negatively. If, after becoming aware of such irrationality, you choose to alter that IB (irrational belief) and replace it with an RB (rational belief), you may find that your reactions become much less negative, and in some cases indifferent or even positive.

In the example cited earlier, when someone speaks badly of you, you experience a negative feeling. Why? What is your perception, judgement, or belief "behind" this negative reaction? You are perhaps assuming, at a subconscious level, that "everyone in this world must like me, or even love me;" or that "everyone should speak nicely about me;" or that "no one should dislike me, or speak nastily about me," and so on. However, return to reality, and ask yourself: Do *you* like or love everyone in this world? Do you dislike anyone? Do you always speak well about everyone? Do you never speak ill about anyone?

Realistically, factually, or rationally speaking, is it not true that you do not like or love everyone in this world? You do dislike some people and possibly you do not speak well about everyone all the time. You may even occasionally speak badly about some people (sometimes, maybe, with pleasure!). If this is so for all of us, then is it realistic or rational to believe or expect that "everyone must like me" or that "no one should speak nastily about me?" In fact the assumption that there are always going to be people who dislike you and speak ill about you is the more realistic or rational belief. If you choose to substitute this RB for the more commonly held IB, there is every likelihood that your reaction to the event of someone speaking badly about you will be less negative or even neutral. The internal dialog you would have with yourself would be as follows "That person might be one of those who is expected to speak nastily about me. There's nothing unexpected, or unusual about it." This is illustrated in Figure 7.5.

In the first instance, referring to Figure 7.5, if you hold an irrational belief at the subconscious level that "nobody should speak badly about me," then the syndrome would be as in (a) – experiencing a negative reaction and behavior. However, if you consciously alter your belief into a more rational one that "there will always be someone who will speak badly about me," then your

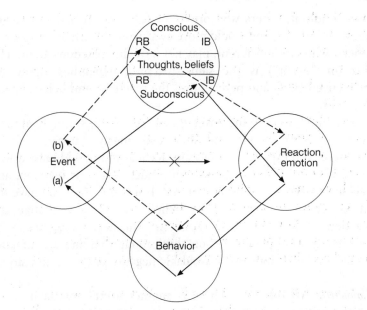

Figure 7.5 Managing Beliefs.

reaction and behavior would most probably be as in (b) – less negative or more positive. The significant point to be noted is that the event is the same, but your reaction is different in situation (b). This in turn enables you to behave more proactively, instead of the more reactive behavior resulting from a negative reaction from the IB in situation (a).

The most important thing to realize is that the event is the same and yet, in this way, you can manage your negative feelings effectively. We have a perennial mental chatter or dialog going on within us. This arises from our belief system which perceives, interprets, and judges the events surrounding us, creating certain expectations, which when unfulfilled or violated, cause the negative reactions within us. Despite our intelligence and wisdom, there are a number of irrational beliefs stored within us, at a more basic level than we would like to "believe."

A simpler illustration of this point, that our reactions are subjective or relative to our own personal beliefs, is the following, relating to dogs. Some people love dogs, some hate them, or are afraid of them, and some are indifferent: these are all subjective attitudes. Therefore, in the presence of a dog, a dog lover would experience positive feelings, and probably move close to it, and even fondle it; others who dislike or fear dogs would experience negative feelings, and would move away from the animal; and some others, who are indifferent, may not have any reactions at all. The dog (or "event") is the same whereas, depending upon our subjective beliefs and perceptions, the reactions and behaviors are different.

Therefore, to curb the onset of negative feelings, you need to be aware of your beliefs and then consciously "manage" them. Whenever you experience a negative feeling, you should immediately relate it to the belief or judgement underlying your reaction, and decide whether it is valid or justified. If it is not, then you have the choice either to change your belief, and thereby change the reaction, or to continue to experience the negative feeling. Unfortunately, most people do not "think about what they are thinking about," and therefore suffer avoidable negative emotions and stress.

2 *Converting RB into PB*   There is another useful approach to the management of beliefs, that of converting rational beliefs (RB) into more practical or pragmatic (PB) ones. It is not only because of your irrational beliefs that you experience negative feelings. There are situations in which your thinking or beliefs are quite rational and justified. For example, when a friend is ill you feel anxious, or when you want something and subsequently fail to get it, you feel disappointed. There is nothing irrational in this. The problem is that the intensity of your negative reactions is frequently far beyond what may be considered to be "reasonable." In such a case you tend to exaggerate your reactions, which has an undesirable impact on your feelings, health, and performance.

There are two dimensions to the management of your rational beliefs. Firstly, there are situations or things that are vital to your existence. These can be described as your survival "needs," such as food, fresh air, water, and shelter, at the physiological survival level, nonfulfillment of which is a disaster. Similarly, at the sociological, or emotional, level, we "need" only a few relationships for emotional survival, and a few recognitions or achievements at the psychological level. Secondly, there are things that you want, but which are not essential for your existence. These may be good to have, but are not "necessities." In other words, they are niceties. If these needs are not fulfilled it will not be a "disaster" but, more realistically, an "inconvenience." This is illustrated in Figure 7.6.

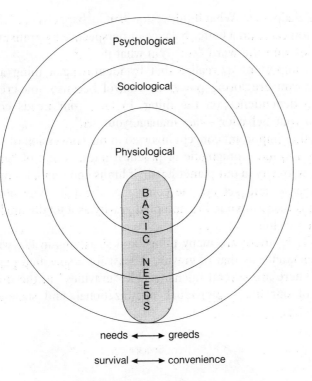

needs ←——→ greeds

survival ←——→ convenience

Figure 7.6 Basic Needs.

On careful reflection, you should be able to identify at the various levels – physiological, sociological, and psychological – which are your survival needs and which are the "niceties," or even greeds. Unfortunately, we tend to get upset far more frequently and intensely than is necessary, even when one of the "niceties" is not fulfilled, and behave as if this represented the nonfulfillment of a "need" or "necessity." To the extent that you are able to clearly distinguish your needs from your niceties, and subsequently adopt a balanced approach, you can derive two concrete benefits. Firstly, with such clarity and awareness, the nonfulfillment of "niceties" will not upset or disappoint you so much. Secondly, your sense of satisfaction with, and enjoyment of, the large number of "niceties" that you possess or enjoy will grow significantly. The enjoyment will be further enhanced by the fact that, with such a "pragmatic" approach, your "fear of losing" your "possessions" or "positions" will also be reduced significantly.

We frequently suffer unnecessary anxiety, resulting from such mental dialogs as "What if this . . . or that . . . happens . . .?" In such cases you can gain a better balance or perspective by prefixing such anxieties with the word "so:" "So what if . . .?"

It is important to realize that by identifying a thing as your "need" you are losing power or control because you create an intense dependence on the thing. In fact, your needs come to control your behavior – *they* manage your self!

Another important concept involved in the conversion of rational beliefs into more pragmatic or practical ones, is that of "gravity." There is gravity in our planet Earth: it limits and regulates our lives significantly, and yet no one complains about it. Why not? The reason is that everyone has accepted gravity as a totally unchangeable fact of life.

Similarly, there are many things and situations in life with the same character as that of gravity, at least for a specified period of time. There are several unchangeable "gravities" in the different levels of our life – individual, organizational, and societal (see Figure 7.7).

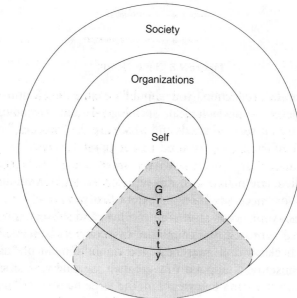

Figure 7.7 Gravities.

For example, at the individual or personal level there are several physical aspects, or features of your body, that cannot be changed during your entire life, and some, for example weight, which are not changeable for a specified period – of, say, one year, three months, one week, or even one day. Moreover, there are similar changeable or nonchangeable "gravities" in other dimensions of your mental and emotional self, either for your entire lifetime or over a specific period of time.

The same applies at the organizational and societal levels. You frequently become agitated over things or situations that are unchangeable within a particular time frame. You fritter away your energies and resources trying to change such "gravities." There are several other things and situations which you can influence and change, but if your attention and energies are engaged in such a dysfunctional way, the effectiveness of your efforts in other areas will be seriously and adversely affected. You need to identify explicitly at various levels – personal, organizational, and societal – what are "gravities" within a particular time frame and what are not. This will enable you to make more judicious use of your resources. Then, by setting proper priorities you can, over a period, maximize the desired change and minimize the "gravities" around you. This approach does not imply a passive or fatalistic acceptance of everything. Quite the contrary. It implies that if you want to be effective in your "change" strategies, you have to apply your limited resources in a pragmatic manner, rather than dissipating them on a more emotional or prejudiced basis. That is why the line in Figure 7.7 indicating gravities is a dotted one, not a solid one.

Managing expectations

The second frame of reference for preventing or minimizing negative emotions, is that of managing expectations. You saw earlier how negative stress results from the gap between your expectations and their achievement or fulfillment. There are two factors responsible then for your negative feelings, your level of expectation and the level of their fulfillment. On the basis of this realization, we can develop the following "happiness formula:"

$$H \text{ (Happiness)} = A \text{ (Achievement)} \div E \text{ (Expectations)}$$

If our expectation (of results) is zero, even the slightest achievement or fulfillment will result in infinite happiness! (See Figure 7.8.)

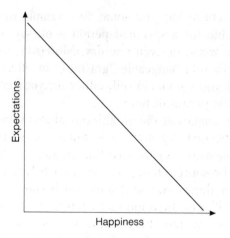

Figure 7.8

It is of the utmost importance, however, to be clear about the meaning of the word "expectation." It does not mean *intention to achieve* or to have motivation, ambition, objectives, or goals. It refers only to *expectation of results* while engaged in the efforts to achieve results. To have "achievement motivation" and to have "results orientation" are different things, and it is vital that you grasp the significance of this difference. You can have an intention to achieve, and make the necessary efforts, without being worried about the fact (while making the efforts) that the result may not ultimately be achieved. In other words, the *attention*, fixation, or psychic investment, is not in the actual realization of results but in making the required efforts to achieve those results.

Results depend on several factors, both internal and external, over which you cannot expect to have full control. There is an inherent uncertainty involved in the actual achievement of results, despite your best intentions and efforts. Therefore, your fixation with, or psychic investment in, the results *per se* causes an unnecessary degree of anxiety and tension while making the effort to achieve them. This would affect your performance adversely. Rather, once you have clearly established your goals or targets, you should pay full attention to your efforts or to the process which can lead to the result. In this way, you can concentrate better and give full attention to the process of achieving, without "worrying" about the end result. You thereby perform better, and therefore increase the probability of achieving the result – action and performance flow. Expectation of results, while making the efforts, inevitably generates a fear of not achieving the results – a "fear" of "losing" – which is dysfunctional for results.

With such an attitude or approach, you would in fact enjoy the "process" much more. This would also then contribute to your performance and finally to the end result. But here lies a subtle paradox. By remaining detached from the expectation of actual results, while keeping in touch with your intentions and commitment to them, you give greater attention and energy to your efforts. As a consequence you are not only more successful but you do not incur negative emotions, tensions, frustrations, or stress. In fact, you experience full joy and satisfaction all the time. This success and satisfaction emerge from pursuing your objectives with "detached involvement." Functioning with such detachment from results and involvement with efforts is called "*management by detached involvement.*"

I shall now give a somewhat simplistic example to illustrate this. When you have to visit a building on a very busy street, where you know it is almost impossible to get a parking space, you have hardly any expectation of finding one. But while driving toward that building you will still be looking for a parking space near the building (just in case!), and if you do find a space right in front of the building, what will your reaction be? Generally, it will be one of positive excitement or happiness. In this case, the expectation of a result (finding a parking space) was zero; therefore, in a sense, happiness was infinite!

Consider the opposite situation: suppose you are driving toward a suburban destination where you know there will not be any difficulty in finding a parking space. Therefore your expectation of finding it is 100 percent. On reaching your destination, however, for some extraordinary reason you find cars parked all around the place, with not a single space available for you in the vicinity. What is your reaction in this case? Almost inevitably, it is anger, frustration, unhappiness, and stress! In both cases, it was your attitude or expectation that made the difference to your emotions.

Here is a deeper, more subtle example. Each participant in a marathon has every intention and desire to win. However, imagine that there are two contenders who have different approaches or expectations. The mental dialog in the mind of participant A, just before he starts to run, is:

I am here to win this race. The only way I can win this race is to reach the winning line first, before anyone else does. The only way I can do so is to remain ahead of the others all the time and that will be my unremitting focus [expectation].

The mental dialog of participant B is:

I am here to win this race. The only way I can win is to reach the winning line first, before anyone else does. The only way I can do so is to do my best, run my fastest, and that will be the focus of my attention all the time.

Note the identical intentions. However, there is a crucial difference between the two attitudes/expectations. A's focus is on the result "staying ahead of the others all the time," whereas B's focus is on the effort "Doing my best, running my fastest."

Assuming that the running ability of both A and B is the same, who is likely to win? In response to such a question, most managers are almost evenly divided between A and B. However, some may suggest that some other participant, C, might win the race, being a better runner than both!

Let us consider the possibilities in the case of A. Because he wants to stay ahead of the others all the time, his attention and energy will to some extent be diverted to "observing" others and their performance. Even if he is ahead to start with, he may have an anxiety about others closing in. In fact, in almost all long races, the ultimate winner is not always in front. Runner A will feel a growing level of anxiety whenever any other participant gets closer to him; this will intensify if someone is "neck and neck" with him. Finally if someone gets ahead of him – which can and does happen – he may feel even demoralized. A considerable amount of negative emotion or tension will be experienced by A, resulting in a significant amount of "energy leakage," affecting his performance adversely.

However, it is quite possible that the "fear of losing" may sometimes generate more adrenalin in A, and that this could trigger much faster running. Runner A may even overtake the others once again. But such a thrust is likely to be temporary, and within a short time because of adrenalin he will be exhausted, and not be able to run even at his normal pace; therefore ultimately he may lose. If you put a tiger behind someone, he will run far beyond even his peak level because of the "fear of losing" (his life!), but only for a short time. In your job, and in your life, you are not interested only in short-term performance or gain, but in sustainable, peak performance.

Suppose that B or even C wins; that is, A loses. In such a case what is A's reaction likely to be? Mostly, it would be frustration and perhaps even depression.

Most importantly, what is the experience of A, his mental state, during the process of running? As noted above, because his psychic investment is in the "result," he is likely to experience a constant undercurrent of anxiety, fear of losing, and of not achieving the result. Therefore his mental state is likely to be tense throughout the running process.

What is the position of B, then, in the same three situations discussed above? Because his focus is on doing his best, B's attention and energy will be totally absorbed in achieving his full potential in running. He is fully aware that he is engaged in a competitive race, and that the only purpose of his being there is to win. But his attention is not disturbed or unduly diverted by the performance of others.

Even if A or C wins the race, B's reaction will be more in the nature of "I really did my best – that is all I could do anyway. But my best was not good enough. Now let me find out how I can better my best." That is a positive, constructive approach.

Finally, what is B's experience while running? Because of his concentration in doing his best, and in achieving peak performance, he is absorbed in his running, in almost a "flow" state. In a sense he "becomes" or identifies himself with running. We perform much better when we are free of anxiety or tension, and particularly when we enjoy the process – it becomes almost effortless. Taking an example from the performing arts, even a maestro, a musician, or a dancer is at his best when he is totally absorbed in performance. He "becomes" the music or dance: there is no consciousness at that time that he is performing or that there is any critical audience. He thereby creates the context in which peak performance shows up. Such *peak performance* is, in such a situation, also a *peak experience*. B has no fear of losing while running, as his expectation is not focused on winning or on results, but only on the process – on making his best effort. With A's attitude, however, with an expectation of or attachment to results, you are most likely to operate from a fear of losing, resulting in tension and stress. With B's attitude, with the *intention* to win, but with your *attention* focused on effort, without attachment to *result*, you are most likely to operate on the basis of a "joy of doing." A would be "worrying," whereas B is absorbed in "running." In order to win we do not have to win the "fight" – we have to win the "fighting" or fight the "winning" (expectation of results).

However, you must recognize that in a short race, even if you operate out of fear, with adrenalin-generated energy, you can win the "race." But you will feel exhausted. This may be peak performance, but not peak experience! In business, you frequently find managers following such an approach, with the consequent frustration and growing psychosomatic illnesses. In other words, you or I become "success-fools." If the culture of any organization is focused on short-term or quarterly targets, it would produce sick people for a healthy company!

Your life, your career, or your job is, then, a long, ongoing race. Moreover, life is a journey, not a destination! The process of reaching, therefore, becomes more important than the event of arriving. You are not likely to be interested in a few, temporary successes or gains. Therefore, if you want to achieve durable, sustainable success, without stress and with satisfaction, you need to manage your expectations. Above all, you need to be able to differentiate between your "intention to achieve" and your "expectation of results." The paradox is that to ensure the achievement of a result you need to be detached from it! Your full and undivided attention is then devoted to action, to performance. This ensures achievement of the desired result. Sustainable peak performance occurs only when it coincides with peak experience, which is facilitated by detached involvement.

Managing comparisons

Just as the gap between your expectations and their fulfillment causes negative emotions, so the gap between what you have and what (you perceive) others have, or between what you have and what you want to have, also causes negative emotions within you. The existence and the extent of the gap is dependent upon your *perception* of what you have and what others have, as well as on your criteria for comparison.

There is a common tendency to overestimate what others possess and underestimate what you have. There are several psychological and cultural reasons for such self-depreciating behavior. You need to be aware of this, and make a constant effort to correct such a tendency, along with the process of developing more realistic perceptions.

I can illustrate this point using a well known diagram:

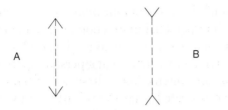

The two lines, A and B, are of exactly the same length. Yet because of the way in which the arrows at the top and the bottom are positioned, setting the context, your perception of the lengths of these lines changes. Line B appears to be longer than line A. Our general tendency is to view "what others have" as line B and what we have as line A. If and when you experience negative feelings of envy and frustration, as a result of such comparisons, and this triggers off a continuing competitive pressure, you need to watch out and manage such comparisons at two levels:

1 at a *philosophical* level, where we have to sort out within our selves how much and how far we want to manage our lives on the basis of comparisons with others; and
2 at a *commonsense* level, where we have to ensure that the comparisons are made with a proper and realistic perspective and perceptions. Hell has been sometimes described as imagining movies of what life could have been! It would therefore be worthwhile to remember in any comparisons that "it could be worse."

Managing life positions/ego states: transactional analysis

As stated earlier, there are several psychological reasons for a common tendency known as "self knocking." One of the theories expounded by Dr Eric Berne, namely "transactional analysis" (TA), deals with this in an elaborate manner. TA offers a useful conceptual framework for the management of your "life positions" and "ego states," being simultaneously a theory of personality, a model of social interactions, and a mode of therapy.

Put in simple terms, the objective of TA is to help normal people to understand their "moods and modes," as well as those of others, better. As a result they can prevent or minimize negative reactions, and facilitate more proactive and appropriate behavior, performance, and "transactions."

A "transaction" is a communication or interaction, verbal or nonverbal. Any interpersonal transaction implies interaction between the minds, or mental states, of individuals involved in the transaction. There are different mental states that a person experiences, or passes through, during any interaction. These are classified by Dr Eric Berne into three so-called "ego states," namely the super ego, the ego, and the id, or the parent, adult, and child, respectively, as shown in Figure 7.9.

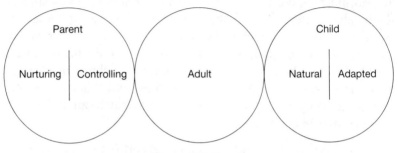

Figure 7.9 Ego States.

Each ego state represents a particular state of mind, intention, or mood. The "adult" state is an information-giving or -receiving one: no opinions or emotions are transacted. The "child" state is the emotional one, like that of a child. Each one of us, however old we may be, still has elements of our "childhood" within us. So you frequently act or react in such a (child-like) "natural" and "innocent" or "rebellious" (childish) way. Finally, you have strong imprints in your mind, called a "script" in TA terms, of your experiences and interactions with your parents, including both kind, caring, and nurturing ones, as well as judgemental, controlling, and critical ones.

Therefore, there are five major states or moods from which you could be operating or transacting. The "parent" (P) could be (1) nurturing or (2) critical. The "adult" (3) engages in information exchange. Finally, the "child" could be (4) natural (spontaneous) or (5) adaptive (compliant), in either case being emotionally expressive.

Depending upon the ego state from which you are operating, communication (the transaction) can be either complementary or crossed, as shown in the "transograms" of Figures 7.10 and 7.11.

Here are some very simple examples.

1 A "complementary transaction" which generates a positive response: *Question*: "What is the time?" (adult ego state)

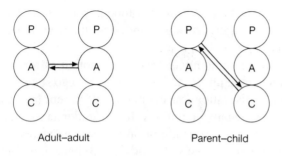

Figure 7.10 Complementary Transactions.

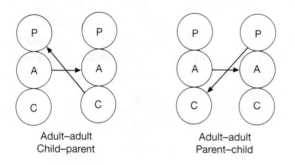

Figure 7.11 Crossed Transactions.

Response: "The time is now ten-thirty." (adult ego state)
2 A "crossed transaction" which generates negative emotion:
Question: "What is the time?" (adult)
Response: "Why don't you keep your own watch. . . ." (critical parent)

The relevance of TA, in the context of managing negative emotions, is that the ego state from which you are likely to operate depends, to a great extent, upon the "life position" you have adopted. In broad terms, there are four possible life positions that you can adopt, while interacting with another person:

1 "I'm OK, you're OK" – confident
2 "I'm not OK, you're OK" – archaic
3 "I'm OK, you're not OK" – superior
4 "I'm not OK, you're not OK" – hopeless

There are several reasons why you might adopt one or other of these life positions. For example, a possible reason for adopting an "I'm not

OK" position is that, during childhood, you found that everyone around you was bigger, stronger, and wiser than you were – or so you were led to believe.

A considerable amount of negative emotion is involved in your adopting such a life position. The consequent ego state may be that of an "adapted" child (submissive) or "critical" parent (aggressive), both of whom carry negative emotions. If you understand such concepts, and become aware of your life positions and ego states, you can also understand other people's "moods" and behaviors better. Such awareness and use of various concepts described in this book will enable you to manage your ego states, transactions and emotionally based interactions with more positive emotions and success. Particularly, the use of the "Centering" exercise (see page 99) is most effective in shifting among ego states lucidly and instantly.

Transactional analysis is, in fact, very elaborate and complex: we have only touched upon its most elementary principles with a view to emphasizing their relevance and significance. In its fuller form it is one of the most useful approaches for managing negative emotions.

Managing worries

Practically everyone has worries, big or small, at any given moment. But do you worry "efficiently"? As part of a professional approach to the management of self, you can develop a more systematic approach to the managing of or dealing with worries, to minimize the experience of negative emotions. There are four steps involved in this "professional" management of worries.

1 *Devise worry breaks* The wide range of worries that you experience are so pervasive that they can remain as a chronic and continuing undercurrent, popping up at any time during the day or night. They interrupt your thinking processes, create emotional disturbances, and distort your concentration in whatever you may be involved with at that time. Unfortunately, even if you try to prevent or block such "worries" you will not succeed. This is because, at the mental level, *whatever we resist has a tendency to persist.* It interferes with your concentration and therefore with your performance. And because you are busy most of the time, always having more to do than the time

available in which to do it, you do not spend sufficient time in thinking these worries through. The process becomes a vicious spiral.

To break that spiral, you should create "worry breaks." You have already integrated coffee breaks and lunch breaks into your daily routine. Similarly, you need to give yourself sufficient time to think about your worries. For a week or two, even on an experimental basis, you should plan a regular daily break, during your work routine, at a specified time for 30 minutes or so. This may be reduced as and when sufficient systematic "worrying" has already been done.

2 *Create a master list*   On the first day, at the beginning of the worry break, you should start by making a master list of all the worries. The listing should be made in whatever sequence they appear in your mind. Let all the worries, big and small, be poured out onto a sheet of paper, without any kind of mental screening.

3 *Prioritization*   After an exhaustive master list of all the worries has been made, each should be classified according to two parameters:

(a) *Likelihood*. Worries are usually about some events occurring or not occurring. Different events may be more or less likely to occur. There is a spectrum of probabilities, ranging from most "likely" to most "unlikely."
(b) *Seriousness*. For each worry, estimate the degree of seriousness of the consequences of the event, from "serious" to "not serious." These two parameters could be plotted on the "worry worksheet," as shown in Figure 7.12. Each of the worries from the master list should be grouped in one of the appropriate quadrants. Worries in quadrant A would have the highest priority.

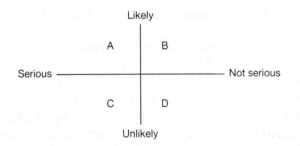

Figure 7.12 Worry Worksheet.

4 *Action plan*   On the basis of this prioritization of worries, develop an appropriate action plan for each worry. Prioritization should also

be reviewed during every worry break, because situations keep changing.

As a result of such a sequential process, four things are likely to happen:

1 The very act of preparing a master list, of putting all the worries on paper, results in considerable relief! Moreover, it is quite likely that you find that, after all, you do not have that many serious worries. This creates a sense of relief and reduces a considerable amount of negative emotion. Sometimes it may happen that you find you have far more problems or worries than you expected. If this happens, it is even more important that you become aware of the real situation and begin to do something about it!

2 By prioritization, appropriate and timely action is taken, which also reduces the worries and negative emotions.

3 This process "clears up" the constant "noise" in your system. As there is a specific time allocated for "worrying," worries rarely pop up for your attention at any other time. However, if any worry does pop up at a time when you are concentrating on some other task, you can "tell yourself" (quite seriously!) that it will receive your attention during the next worry break! This really works, provided that you do take a daily worry break at the same specified time. If you do not do so, your mind will relapse into its original habit of spreading out the worries into a constant undercurrent, with all the negative consequences. After practising this professional approach regularly for a few days or weeks, you can reduce the duration and frequency of the breaks. The important thing is keep up the process on a regular basis, whatever the predetermined timing and spacing. This may sound odd (perhaps it really is!) but it does work!

4 Apart from such management of worries reducing your level of negative emotion, this also reduces your propensity to worry. It seems that most of us have formed a habit of perceiving problems, or "a propensity to problemise." If someone were to eliminate half of your problems, or worries, there is a strong likelihood that you would add the same number of problems, so as to maintain your level of worries or problems at a constant level. We seem to have created a certain "need" or habit for worries or problems. By following the process explained above, you become aware of this, and so gradually downgrade this perverse propensity.

The Curative Level: Dealing with Anger

Despite your best efforts to prevent negative emotions, you may still experience some, as your "management" of emotions may not yet be foolproof.

How do you manage these negative emotions, once they have occurred? One of the most frequently experienced emotions is anger or irritation. The usual approach is either to express or suppress anger. If you express anger, you feel a sense of relief, or satisfaction, at that moment. But, after some time, you frequently feel guilty about your behavior, guilty that you could not "control" yourself and behave with greater restraint or with better manners. You occasionally apologize or "explain" to the individual concerned and then feel better. However, if you keep on controlling and suppressing your anger, for the sake of "appropriate" behavior, over a period of time you may develop ulcers. If you express your anger, you feel guilty; if you suppress it, you feel sick! This is what we call a double bind – you are locked into a kind of "fight" or "flight" response. Expressing anger is, in a sense, a flight response, whereas suppressing anger is a fight response.

Is there any way out of these reactive responses, both of which have adverse consequences? Fortunately, there is a way of dealing with anger and irritation, which is not only very powerful and effective, but also conducive to your personal growth. This is called the "transcending response" or the "witness approach." Whenever you experience anger or any other negative emotion which you want to eliminate, do nothing other than becoming aware of the anger, and accept it – allow it to be there. The amazing paradox is that by becoming aware and accepting it, the process of neutral, passive witnessing eliminates anger. What happens is that whenever you want to observe anything, you have to detach yourself from it; you have to create some "distance" between you and the object observed. To give a rather crude and simplistic example, imagine you are seated on a chair and want to "observe the chair." Can you observe it, see it fully, as long as you are seated on it? It is impossible to do so. You have to get up, out of the chair, and move a short distance away from it before you can observe it fully. Now, apart from being able to observe the chair by getting out and away from it, there is something else that happens to you in this process. As long as you are seated on the chair, your entire physical contour or posture is dependent on, and controlled or "managed" by the chair. Moreover, you cannot move the chair, do anything else to the chair, or "manage" it as long as you are seated on it, and in a sense attached or identified with it. But the moment you get out of the chair, not only can you observe it, but also, in the process, you remove yourself from the chair's control, and achieve control *over* it. Therefore, the process of observing or witnessing creates a psychic distance or detachment from that which you are witnessing. That gives power to you as the observer or the witness.

In effect, you become "nonangry," and therefore can adopt whatever posture or behavior that you like, proactively. Unlike the fight or flight response, of either expressing or suppressing anger, which also creates other negative consequences and tensions, this witnessing approach generates a feeling of relaxation, as well as one of "being in charge." The whole process involves a shift in your identity, or consciousness, from that of experiencing anger, being angry or, in a sense, being anger, to that of a detached observer, looking on from a deeper level of your self or your transcended consciousness.

This skill of witnessing is a part of a *centering* exercise: that of observing, witnessing, or noticing your body (tightness or tensions in the body), mind (flow of thoughts), and emotions. Through this centering process you detach yourself from your body, mind, and emotion – that is, your ego self – and get in touch with your deeper, witnessing self. By repeating this process you go beyond, or transcend, your ego, emerge on a different plane, and increasingly operate from a higher level of consciousness or self. The basic tenet is that you manage that from which you are detached; you are managed by that with which you are attached or identified. You must remember that you are neither your thoughts, nor your beliefs nor your feelings or behavior: you are the manager of all these. However, if you identify yourself with them you will find it almost impossible to alter them: any effort to do so would imply attacking your self-identity.

Another analogy, even if a somewhat crude one, can be used to explain the essence of this "witnessing" process. When you are driving a car and you have to go uphill, you have to "shift" the gear of your car to a lower, more powerful position. Why do you have to do that? The reason is to enable the car to adjust, or increase its power, so that it can climb up the hill. If you do not shift the gear, what happens? The car will stall and then stop. Similarly, when you find yourself in a difficult situation, or dealing with a difficult person, and you experience anger or any other negative emotion, you need to shift "gears." In other words, you need to change your identity, your consciousness, and operate from that more powerful level. You may think that it would be difficult to become fully involved in a situation and at the same time engage in the witnessing process or contemplate shifting "gears." However, to pursue the analogy, when you learn to drive you are often overwhelmed by the variety of activities involved: keeping an eye on the traffic, regulating the speed, steering the car, operating the car, and operating the brakes and gears. Yet, within a few weeks, you get used to all this and, within a few months, these activities become almost automatic. So, while driving you are not only able to attend to the numerous activities and controls but also to carry on a complex conversation with someone in the car. Similarly, in "witnessing" your negative emotions, just like watching over all the processes involved in driving, you develop expertise over a period of time. Whenever you begin to feel anger (or any other negative emotion which you wish to remove or reduce), you automatically begin to "witness" it and shift away from it.

In this context, it is also important to realize that any resistance to a negative emotion in fact makes it persist. On this basis, the formula for misery would be: M (misery) $= NE$ (negative emotion) $\times R$ (resistance). If the resistance is zero, misery also becomes zero. As discussed earlier, noticing, witnessing, and allowing eliminates the negative emotion.

The Symptomic Level: Dealing with Physical Symptoms

Despite your best efforts to manage negative emotions, there may be occasions when you cannot help but experience intense negativity. These experiences invariably lead to physiological symptoms such as those described earlier: headaches, tightness in the chest, and discomfort in the stomach.

There is a simple "visualization" process which can help to eliminate such psychosomatic symptoms. In the case, say, of a headache, sit in a relaxed posture with your eyes closed and try to visualize your headache. Ask the following questions: Where is the headache in my head: at the back of the head, or the front, or the sides? What is the total area affected in my head? What is its length, breadth, and height? What could its weight be? Can I give it a color? These questions enable you to "visualize" the size, weight, and color of your headache. You have to keep asking yourself the same questions again and again, in the same sequence, making sure that you remain relaxed after each round of questions. You will be surprised how your headache gradually disappears, within a few rounds.

In a sense, this process is similar to that of "witnessing" described earlier. As in the case of anger, by noticing or witnessing it, you escape from the anger, and thereby eliminate it. In the case of a headache, by noticing or visualizing it you detach yourself from it. You can then deal similarly with any other psychosomatic pain or discomfort, in any part of your body.

In managing your emotions, at any level, it is important to remember that life is a series of experiences. But experience is not what happens to you, it is what you do with what happens to you. This depends upon your perceptions, beliefs, attitudes, skills, and efforts. Mistaken notions often cause negative emotions. You may not be able to change events, but you can certainly change your attitude toward events. Nothing in this world is significant unless you choose to make it so. Significance is relative and subjective. Feelings are not emotions that happen to you; they are reactions you "choose" to have. Emotion is therefore a choice, not a condition of life. In that sense, you could almost say that misery is optional and "negotiable." Some people believe that they are worthless, and then do everything to prove themselves right. Someone has said that there are those who believe they can and others who believe they can't – both are right! Unfortunately, because of human nature, the nature of the ego, it is "easier" to be miserable than to be blissful. Somehow, most people seem to be willing to renounce their pleasures but not their suffering.

Finally, it is worth remembering two rules of stress management. To the extent that you are able to observe them, you should never experience negative emotions or stress:

- Rule 1 – never feel stressed about "small stuff"
- Rule 2 – everything is "small stuff"!

There is no stress in the world – there is only stressful thinking. The world is as it is: we make the difference! Angels fly because they take themselves lightly!

We now turn to neurosensory activity.

8

Managing Your Neurosensory System

Neurosensory Activity

The fourth and the most subtle dimension of your self, besides the
body, mind, and emotion, is your nervous system and your five senses.
The interaction between the two (neurosensory) and between them
and the environment, determines the human experience.

Every second, there are about 30,000 stimuli that bombard your
senses from the environment. But, because of the limits of your
sensory receptors, you actually "receive" only a very limited amount
of these external stimuli. Moreover, depending upon your dominant
psychological "drive" at the time, you "perceive" or direct your
attention to only a select segment of whatever stimuli your senses can
receive.

Broadly speaking, you have four basic drives: two physical (sexual
and kinesthetic), intellectual, and emotional. Depending upon which
of these drives is dominant at a given moment, your "mind" will
register only that segment of the incoming stimuli which satisfies that
particular drive. For example, when asked who and what you notice
while waiting in an airport lounge, the usual responses range from
"attractive people," "people constantly on the move" (physical) and
different kinds of people (intellectual) to "children" or "people" who
look familiar (emotional).

The "information" that is distilled or filtered through your sensory
receptors and psychological drives, is your "input." This is then
"processed" together with stored "data" in your "memory box,"
consisting of thoughts, images, and beliefs. Such data processing
results in an output, that is to say what you experience, at two levels.

One level is internal, in your body. The other is external, in the form of your behavior, both verbal and nonverbal. In addition, these "outputs" serve partly as "inputs" in the form of "feedback." This continuing and ongoing process of interaction, as illustrated in Figure 8.1, based on your neurosensory activity, is what human experience is about. In other words, neurosensory activity is a kind of a "live wiring" within your self.

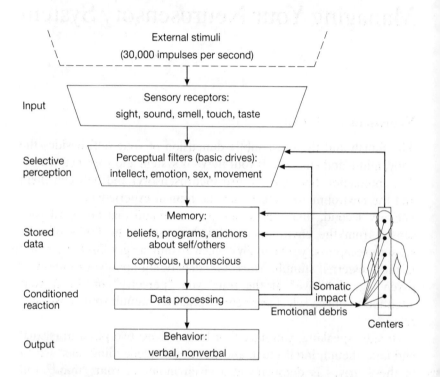

Figure 8.1 The Human Process: Functioning of Your Self.

It is therefore of utmost importance to understand this neurosensory activity, and to develop the skills and competencies to manage the same. This will enable you to manage your experiences, your self, your work, and your life.

The Neurosensory System at Work

The functioning of the central nervous system has already been discussed. The more complex neurosensory activity is illustrated in

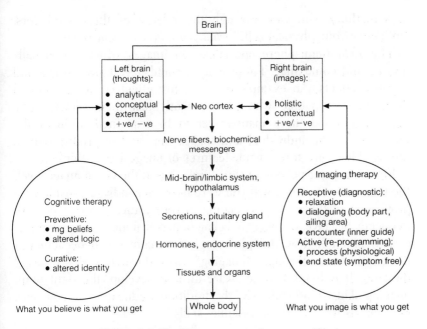

Figure 8.2 The Neurosensory System at Work.

Figure 8.2, which indicates the continuous interaction between body and mind, through neurosensory activity.

The two brain hemispheric functions have already been discussed. As you may recall (see pages 59–61) the *left* hemisphere processes thoughts, which may be analytic or conceptual, and positive or negative, but which relate predominantly to external events. Whatever the nature or profile of your "thinking" may be, it affects your neurosensory system and, through it, your body. If your thoughts have adverse effects, you need to reflect on their content and quality and, if necessary, change or alter them through an "altered logic" approach (see page 80).

Your psychological state affects your physiology through the nervous system. This is the basis of the "placebo effect." If a patient strongly believes in a particular cure, and if a placebo is given instead of the real curative medicine, the patient does get cured. There are chemical molecules, called neuropeptides, which act as neuro-messengers, floating in the fluids of your body. They provide the link between your mind, your immune system, and the body. That link is responsible for the "mind over matter" effect. This is the domain of "psycho-neuro-immunology." In other words, if you strongly believe in something, you can, through the release of these mediators, "influence your physical self:" *what you believe is what you get.*

The *right* hemisphere specializes in images which are usually holistic and contextual. These images could have both positive and negative effects. An example of a negative effect is the accelerated death rate in people who have recently lost their spouse. The depressed mood, in a manner yet to be explained, reduces the immunity of the individual and makes him or her predisposed to illness. There are three major features of image-based thinking.

Firstly, a major portion of your thinking is at the visual image level, the natural level with which you were born. Secondly, a considerable proportion of those images relating to your future performance are frequently negative, or reflect a feeling of personal inadequacy. Thirdly, certain psychological and physiological outcomes can be achieved more effectively through "imaging" than through verbally based thinking. It is helpful to be aware of, and develop, the right-brain imaging skills. Unfortunately, the traditional education system does not help us to learn these essential skills.

Imaging at Work

Here is an example of how much our behavior is influenced by images. Suppose that a wooden plank, which is about 18 inches (approximately 45 cm) wide, and a couple of inches (approximately 5 cm) thick, is placed flat on the floor of a room, and you are asked to walk on it. Would you have any difficulty in doing so? Hardly anyone would have difficulty in performing such an exercise. But imagine that the same plank is now raised about 30 ft (approximately 10 m) above the ground and is held firm by two poles at each end. What would be your response if you were now asked to walk on it? Most people would refuse! Why is this so? What goes through your mind before giving a negative response? It is usually the image of falling. But why do you have the image of falling, and not of walking fearlessly, as you undoubtedly had when your image was of the plank placed firmly on the floor!

If you reflect on this point you will realize, more often than not, that the images which influence your behavior, especially regarding future performance, may be of failure, or at least of inadequate performance. This is what the occurence of "butterflies in the stomach" is about: fear (images) of suboptimal performance in a future event. These "images" are also described as "inner programs." The main issue here is that our behavior is influenced by such programs to the extent that they become self-fulfilling prophecies – they run your life. However, by acquiring imaging skills you can become aware of what your "inner programs" are, and if you wish to change or improve them, you can do so to a significant extent. As a result you will enhance not only your performance, but also your feelings and thoughts.

There is another dimension to imaging, which can be illustrated by the following exercise. Firstly, try and consciously create saliva in your mouth. Take a few moments and now note how much saliva you have been able to generate. Secondly, go through the following imaging exercise with your eyes closed. (You may ask someone to read out the following instructions.)

Imagine a ripe lemon (or any preferred fruit). Even by looking at it, in your imagination, you can feel that it is a ripe and juicy lemon. Imagine that you are picking up this lemon in one of your hands and pressing it a bit. You feel even more intensely that this lemon has a lot of juice in it. Now, hold the lemon close to your nose and take a deep breath and smell it. Experience its strong but fresh fragrance. Then, with the other hand, pick up a knife and begin to slice the lemon. While doing this, a lot of juice trickles out of the lemon onto your fingers. Not only do you experience the strong lemon smell but also the stickiness of the juice, flowing down your fingers and onto your palm. Finally, pick up a slice of the lemon and put it in your mouth, experiencing all the time the fresh, tangy taste filling your senses. Now you may open your eyes and notice how much saliva there is.

Those of you who were able to "image" the lemon vividly would generate a lot more saliva in your mouths than you originally had. Whereas in the first instance you used your left brain, and the somatic pathway of your nervous system (see page 61), in the second instance you used the right brain and the autonomic parasympathetic pathway. Using the appropriate "channel of communication," you can evoke a more effective response from within yourself.

The most important point, however, is that in all this, in order to create an effect – in this case, more saliva – you are not deliberately trying to create saliva. You are simply imaging the lemon, and salivating "happens" to you. You gave yourself an inner, neurosensory experience and saliva happened. It is important to understand this because, in the same way, if you want to generate a certain kind of behavior or feeling, or even certain qualities and competencies in yourself you can do so more effectively by creating a certain kind of inner experience than by cognitive thinking alone.

As you may recall, on page 20 we reviewed the most important quality that you sought in your boss. The qualities identified were "fairness," "understanding," "patience," "generosity," and so on. Such attitudinal qualities, as opposed to knowledge or skill, cannot be acquired, in a genuine sense, just by desiring them, or even by having a deep commitment to acquire them. In fact, you have to alter your inner experience, through management of your neurosensory system, in such a manner that these qualities become the natural consequence, a kind of fragrance or flavor, of such an experience: this is "centering" or getting in touch with your deeper self.

The imaging skills (as in the case of the lemon) help to create this inner experience. Various processes and steps are involved in learning these skills (mentioned in Figure 8.2 under imaging therapy) which are quite simple and easy to cultivate. There are several good books and tapes now available on mental imagery. The message being conveyed here, in summary, is that "what you image is what you get!"

We now turn to the final aspect of your "self" to be managed, your state of consciousness.

9

Managing Consciousness

Levels of Consciousness

So far man has been described as a "rational animal." Now that "rationality" is also found in several other living species, man is distinguished as a "conscious animal" – the only species known so far to be capable of consciously experiencing different levels of consciousness.

We ordinarily recognize three states of consciousness: deep sleep, in which there is no sensory experience; a dream state, in which the content of the dream is the "reality"; and, finally, the ordinary wakeful state.

In ancient Indian thought, the experience of reality is based on the state of consciousness. A detailed description of this concept can be found in an elaborate and comprehensive model, known as the system of energy centers or "chakras," the Kundalini or the spectrum of consciousness. According to this system there are seven energy centers located in a human being, representing seven different levels of consciousness.

The first center, at the base of the spine, is the anal center, described as the *mooladhara*. The second is the genital center, and is described as the *swadhishthana*. The third corresponds to the solar plexus and is called the *manipura*. The fourth or "central" chakra is located near the heart, at the center of the chest, and is called the *anahata*. The fifth is the throat center, or the *vishuddhi*. The sixth is at the center of the forehead, between the eyebrows, and is called the *ajna*. Finally, the seventh and highest "crown" center is *sahasrara*, located at the top of the head.

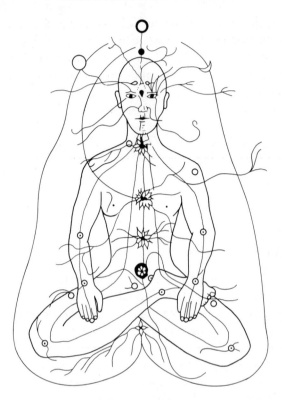

Figure 9.1 The Energy System.

The "chakras" form a comprehensive psycho–neuro system (see Figure 9.1). Each "chakra" or energy center is associated with a certain state of mind or consciousness, and therefore with certain perceptions, attitudes, and experiences.

The first three centers correspond to the Maslovian "need hierarchy." Consciousness at the first-root, or anal-center, is "reptilian" in nature, corresponding to Maslow's physiological survival needs. The second center represents the "mammalian" brain or limbic system, where the predominant need is for emotional stability or satisfaction through affiliation or relationships. This is reflected in Maslow's "need to belong." At the third center, the psychological need for achievement and recognition is dominant. All three of these stages are in the domain of the personal ego.

The fourth, the "heart center" is the stage of entry, or the "threshold," to a higher level of consciousness which goes beyond the ego. Through it you experience "selfless love and compassion." The fifth, the "throat center," relates to creativity and communication; the sixth, sometimes referred to as "the third eye," is the seat of intuition; and the seventh, the crown, is the level of pure, transpersonal or supra-consciousness. The content of each level of consciousness is described in Table 9.1.

Table 9.1 The seven states of consciousness

State of Consciousness	Awareness of self		Awareness of other objects		
			Absolute Level		Relative level
	Individual self	Pure self	Gross	Subtle	
1 Waking	√	—	√	—	—
2 Dreaming	?	—	—	—	—
3 Deep sleep	—	—	—	—	—
4 Transcendental	—	√	—	—	—
5 Lucid awareness	√	√	√	—	—
6 Creative	√	√	√	√	—
7 Cosmic consciousness	√	√	√	√	√

The Nature of Consciousness

Consciousness can be viewed as a form of awareness. There are different levels of awareness ranging from states of waking, dreaming, deep sleep, transcendence, lucid awareness, creativity, to cosmic consciousness, as shown in Table 9.1.

Awareness can be of two types: of the self, and of other objects. Within awareness of your self, you can be aware of both your individual self and of your "being" level or "pure" self. Similarly, awareness of other objects is either absolute or relative. Absolute awareness can exist at a gross or a subtle level.

You find that in your ordinary waking state you are aware of your individual (ego) self and of the gross, absolute levels in other objects: you experience yourself and all other objects as separate discrete entities. In the dream state the reality is the content of the dream. During deep sleep there is no sensory awareness. During meditation (with closed eyes), you are aware of your pure self. During the state of lucid awareness (with open eyes), you become aware of both the individual and pure self, and of the gross level in others. At a creative level you gain a subtle awareness of others. This implies that you perceive any other objects not only as separate absolute entities, but also as a manifestation of the same energy which is the common denominator in everything. At the cosmic level, you experience yourself as an expression of the cosmic consciousness, the ultimate reality, like everything else. As a result the whole universe is perceived as an interconnected web of relationships. Your ego self becomes dissolved into such cosmic awareness, and you perceive and experience reality at all levels and in all its manifestations.

For each of these states of consciousness, or centers (chakras), there are also vibrations which can be associated with certain sounds, as well as with certain colors. There are various types and processes of meditations which enable you to activate or awaken each of these centers. Such awakening generally takes place sequentially in an ascending order. When all the centers of the entire chakra system are awakened, an almost inexhaustible flow of energy is generated. This enables a human being to experience states of consciousness far beyond what is described as the ordinary wakeful state.

Meditation: A Vital Skill for Managing Consciousness

Meditation is a mental process which enables us to be aware of, access, and achieve different levels of mind and states of consciousness or awareness. It is like tuning an instrument: "readying it for playing." It enables you to generate an inner state or context in which not only you experience a joyous energy, but also open up a flow of intuitive knowing.

There are innumerable approaches to meditation, which can be grouped, broadly speaking, into five categories:

- Concentration:
  - sense objects (images, sounds, words)
  - breath
  - chakras (energy centers)
- Contemplation:
  - ethics
  - qualities, virtues
  - ancestors
- Awareness:
  - active (sense perceptions, body parts, sensations)
  - passive (thoughts, emotions)

- Imaging:
  - forms
  - colors
  - transformations of shapes and colors
  - guided imagery, fantasies, dreams
- Transcendental:
  - mantra, sound
  - pure consciousness

Another way of classifying meditation is on the basis of the different processes involved in each case, encompassing "ascent" or "descent," "preservation," or "release" of consciousness (see Figure 9.2).

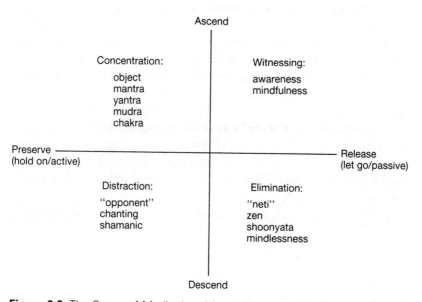

Figure 9.2 The Scope of Meditation: Mental Processes for Altered States of Consciousness.

There are therefore two different dimensions of meditation. Firstly, the approach to meditation can lead either to ascending – toward an awareness of the self – or to descending – negating your self. Secondly, it may lead to experiencing yourself as "everything" or infinity (preservation) or as nothing or zero (release). In the former, the focus is on active concentration on "preservation" of the self or passive reflection on the same. In the latter, the intention is to get "away" from the self through active distraction, or through passive elimination processes. There is a wide variety of meditations relevant to each approach, only a few of which are mentioned in the four quadrants shown in Figure 9.2. Everyone is a unique entity and therefore you may find one or other of the processes more suitable. There are a number of good books now available on various processes of meditation. The ultimate objective and experience in all these approaches and processes is to achieve pure consciousness or nonjudgemental choiceless awareness – just "is-ness." What we are looking for is what is "looking!"

What is the significance of all this, which seems quite remote, for your daily management routines? In fact, your experiences in work and life are related to your state of consciousness. At a practical level, as shown in Figure 9.3, you can see that the stimuli from the external environment are received in your mind, through your senses. However, your specific reaction, or response, in and from your mind, will depend on the "quality" or level of your consciousness. You can group these responses, at an operational level, into three categories: reactive, proactive, and inactive. At the normal reactive level your responses are egocentric and stressful. Conversely, if you are able to access, perhaps through meditation, the deeper level of consciousness described earlier, you can tune your mind into a more proactive level. You then are able to manage through "detached involvement," thereby operating more from the "joy of doing" rather than from the stressful fear of losing.

To be able to manage in this way you would need to regularly

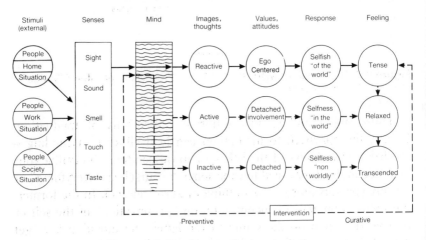

Figure 9.3 The Human System in Action.

practice meditation – using whichever approach you find most suitable – preferably for 15 minutes or so, twice a day. You should do it once in the morning, as a kind of preventive intervention, as shown in Figure 9.3, so that you can begin the day at a proactive level. However, because of a variety of stressful situations during the day, you may easily regress into a reactive ego-dominated stressful posture. It is therefore desirable to meditate again in the evening, to regain your relaxed proactive consciousness. This will serve to reinforce an optimum level of consciousness. Such an optimal outlook – detached involvement – in fact provides the missing link between what you want to do and what you are actually able to, between your knowledge and skills and your performance and results. By remaining in touch with a deeper level of consciousness, you access your deeper potential and, by remaining detached from the "results" while making efforts (and therefore detached from the fear of failure), you achieve higher performance.

This "proactive" state of consciousness is also described as "lucid awareness," remaining in touch with your deeper level of self, while functioning through your "ego" or reactive self. Your inner self is your "inner music" – a constant flow or fountain of joy, energy, and intuition detached from the narrow, selfish identification with the ego, a constant source of fear, regret, guilt, and frustration. A suitable metaphor would be that you remain in touch with the perennial sunshine above the clouds, while managing the activity and storms in and below the clouds, without being affected by them. The quality of your life experience and behavior depends upon the quality of your thinking and the focus of your attention which, in turn, depend upon the level of your consciousness. Deeper consciousness changes not only the chemistry of your mind but also of your body.

The key to this approach of "management by detached involvement" is its win–win nature. You do not suppress your ego nor your ego related needs and aspirations. On the contrary, you enable it to grow, mature, and dissolve by not identifying yourself with it. In your work and life, you remain fully interested and involved in all your pursuits, without being addicted or imprisoned by them. You control or manage that from which you are detached, whereas you become managed or controlled by that to which or with which you are attached or identified!

We now move away from self consciousness, in its individual and managerial perspective, toward self and society, in its broader and societal perspective.

PART III

Self Management in Society

10

Your Self in Society

So far, I have discussed the "dimensions" of the self, and how to "manage" them internally. I have not yet explored what the "self" is in a wider social context. I shall begin, therefore, by describing the overall and evolutionary context in which you can position yourself, as an individual or as a manager, in contemporary society.

The Changing Social Scenario

Present Shock

In his book *Future Shock*, Alvin Toffler has explained the nature of technological and social change very dramatically. If you take 62 years as the average lifetime of a human being, you could then say that during the past 50,000 years the human race has lived about 800 lifetimes. Of these 800 lifetimes the first 650 were spent in caves, the past 70 saw the development of written communication, and it is only in the past six lifetimes that we have the printed word. In the past four lifetimes the measurement of time became possible, and in the very last two the electric motor was invented. But it is in our present lifetime that all the current goods and services we enjoy today have been developed.

If you plot a curve of this progress you will notice an almost vertical line in the past 60 years. The rate of change and the number of events and choices around you have multiplied exponentially. Today, in the developed world, where we seem to find the maximum amount of stress, people face a "tyranny of choices," and a relentless pressure of events. This pace of *quantitative* change has created what could be described as "stressflation."

Qualitative Change

Looking at the evolutionary history of *qualitative* change, you will find that, during the mid-1700s, there was an agricultural revolution. From the mid-1700s to the mid-1900s the industrial revolution ensued, and from the mid-1900s we have been going through a technological revolution. And now, as you approach the end of this century, you find yourself in midst of an information revolution. For that reason contemporary society is also described as an information or innovation society. Now we are even looking beyond the present toward a "post-modern society" in the 21st century.

What has the impact of all this been on us human beings, on our perceptions of "reality," our concepts of our "selves," our values, and our ways of behavior? Moreover, what has been the impact on the way we need to manage ourselves to achieve sustainable peak performance, to acquire leadership qualities, and to secure the competencies needed to transform organizations?

The Failure of Success

While the world has progressed scientifically, technologically, and economically, the individual as a human being seems to have regressed in specific ways, despite his or her phenomenal intellectual and material progress. As a result of the industrial and technological revolution and the consequent mass production and consumption system, the individual has become overspecialized and more standardized. Owing to the prevailing socio-economic system, the growing impact of mass media largely dominated by commercial interests, and the absence of any significant inputs of enlightened values from the education system or the family culture, most individuals, especially in the developed countries (developing countries are not far behind), seem to have become more alienated, "disposable" and even insecure.

One may describe this ironic situation as a "failure of success." In the midst of unprecedented scientific and techno-economic achievements, we have a culture which is predominantly acquisitive and adversarial. Many people, including senior managers, find themselves trapped in this culture, and consequently suffer from the pursuit of heightened sensory gratification as well as selfish attitudes. A high standard of living implies better things: a high standard of life presupposes better "thoughts." We have learnt how to split the atom, but not yet how to unite the world; we have also learnt how to reach the stars – but not each other! What is important here is not to take satisfaction by just joining the chorus, and repeating the "slogans," but to identify the causal factors that have led us into the present crisis, and articulate some effective and practical suggestions for bringing about the desired changes.

Managing Change: The Role of the Manager

How can you "manage" the process of change so as to bring about a constructive synthesis between science and values? The role of the manager, in this respect, is pivotal. As I indicated earlier, as a manager, whether you are aware of it or not and whether you like it or not, you are responsible in a significant way for the current economic and social situation, as well as for bringing about the required changes. You also have the position, power, and resources to do so.

The paradox about change is that, at one level, people want change and, at the same time at another level, they resist it – they fear the loss of what they have which has given them security and comfort. To overcome this you have to consider change not as a "loss" but an "exchange" – giving up what you are for what you could be. An interesting metaphor is about the narrow-mouthed pots full of nuts which are sometimes used to trap monkeys in a forest. The monkeys, lured by the nuts, put their hands in the pots and grab the nuts. But now, with the hands expanded due to the holding of the nuts, the monkeys are unable to withdraw their hands from the mouth of the pot. They remain stuck like this and get captured because they are unwilling to let go of some of the nuts!

The essential thing that is required from you is an appropriate insight into the current situation, set within the context of a deepened perception of "reality," and for you to manage yourself and your surroundings accordingly. This will enable you not only to contribute to bringing about the necessary changes at a societal level, but also to cultivate your own full potential, develop leadership qualities, and help transform your organization, and through it, the entire society. It is the individual drops that make an ocean.

Perceptions of Reality

Reality is what each person makes of it, and that becomes the context from which you operate. It influences your values, thinking and behavior. If you are a manager your concept of reality affects your ideas of your "position" in life, of the role of business, of organizational culture, your management style, and finally your role as a manager.

It is therefore important to grasp the concept and nature of reality, as it forms the fundamental ground and framework for managing your self.

Realms of Perception

On the basis of your differing perceptions, viewpoints, and experiences you offer different descriptions of "reality." It is important to understand the main ones. However, you should be clear that these are only descriptions or "maps" and "models" of reality, and that reality itself may be something else. Your view of reality is based on the experience of that part of reality which you are in touch with.

The fable of the blind men examining an elephant illustrates this well. Each one described the animal on the basis of the part he examined or touched. The animal was identified as a snake, a tree trunk, a rope, and a fan, depending on whether it was the trunk, the leg, the tail, or the ears that they touched.

Each of these people was right. Each one had interpreted reality on the basis of his or her own separate and special experiences.

But because none of them was in touch with the entire elephant nobody was able to comprehend or describe the "total" reality. The process of comprehending reality is, in a sense, a filtration or distillation process. The experiences of reality in your ordinary state of consciousness is based, primarily, on the various sensory inputs that you receive from the part of the environment with which you are in touch.

The method you use to interpret reality, literally and visually, begins with the lens in the eye revealing what it perceives of the object it beholds. This perception is received through sensory cells, from the rods and cones in the retina to the cells in the brain. This occurs in

DIFFERENT VIEWS OF REALITIES

many stages: through the bipolar and ganglion cells, as well as the lateral geniculate nuclei. The information is processed, along with other sensory inputs that may be available on the particular object. The result of this process, that is, the "cognition" that takes place in your conscious mind, is then regarded by you as reality, as shown in Figure 10.1.

As a result you can never really be sure of what actual reality is: for what you experience as cognition, or your perception of what is reality, is based on a variety of inputs of information, namely your senses and "reference material" in your "memory box." If there is any flaw or shortcoming in any of these, there is a likelihood of distortion in perception or cognition with respect to the reality out there. Reality depends upon what and how you see it, or perceive it. So it depends on the level of your awareness, and how much you contaminate the "universal reality" with your "individual projection," as shown in Figure 10.2.

Alternative Realities

You as an observer are the intermediary between reality or "the fact" and observed "facts." While there could be a variety of ways by which

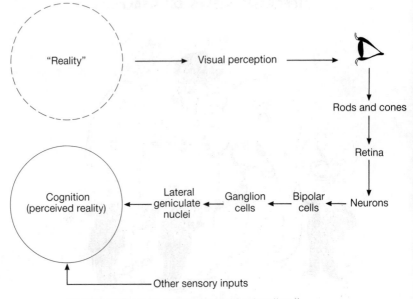

Your "model of reality" depends on what you "see" –
that determines how you "hit the ball". Reality is something else:
visual perception is description of description of description . . . infinite recursion.

Figure 10.1 "Computing Reality": a Filtration/Distillation Process.

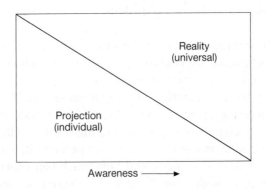

Figure 10.2 Realms of Perception.

you may observe or perceive reality, you basically have "three sets of eyes," consisting of:

• physical or sensory perceptions

- conceptual reasoning
- consciousness-related experience

These can be expanded upon as follows:

Body (flesh)	Mind (brain)	Consciousness (spirit)
sensory perceptions	conceptual reasoning	intuitive
physics	neurosciences	Eastern disciplines
wavicles	holographic	state-specific
space–time–matter	ideas, images, concepts	causal

Physical or sensory perception

On the basis of the first mode of perception, using sensory inputs, or from the standpoint of *physics*, there are basically two different viewpoints: the Cartesian–Newtonian model, and the quantum relativistic model.

The *Cartesian–Newtonian model* based on classical physics describes the universe as a gigantic super-machine, governed by a linear chain of causes and effects. It is a complex mechanical system of interacting discrete particles, and separate objects, and the basic building block is the atom, which is solid matter. Moreover, according to this view, the universe exists objectively in a form which a human observer can perceive and measure. It is also described as a mechanistic and deterministic model of the universe, like a clock. It considers matter as solid, inert, passive, and unconscious. It also believes in a dichotomy of mind and matter. Space is three-dimensional and homogeneous. Time is unidimensional and linear, moving sequentially from past to present to the future.

On the basis of a study of subatomic physics, the *quantum relativistic model* describes the universe as a complex and hierarchial web of interrelationships. The fundamental building blocks are the particles of the atoms (quanta), exhibiting the alternative qualities of matter or energy, depending on how they are viewed. You can perceive reality, then, either as consisting of particles or of waves ("wavicles"). Various objects that you see around you could therefore be perceived as formations of particles/matter or of an interconnected web of energy patterns. Therefore, in this model, the world of substance is replaced by that of process or relationships. Matter disappears into a dynamic vacuum, or pattern. In other words, the universe is perceived as a thought system rather than as a machine. Is a rainbow an object? It exists only because of the unique space-time contextual relationships of the rain, the sun, and you. In this sense you create the rainbow.

Conceptual reasoning

Taking the second mode of perception, based on the findings of the *neurosciences*, the most interesting models are presented by Karl Pribram and David Bohm. Pribram has presented a holographic view of the brain, whereas Bohm has advocated a holonomic view of the universe. What Bohm essentially implies is that the universe consists of two orders, one of which Bohm describes as the explicate or manifest order, and the other as the implicate or nonmanifest order. The manifest order, the world of objects as perceived by our senses is in the nature of a hologram. It is a reflection or representation of the nonmanifest order. Pribram hypothesizes the brain as a hologram. In simplistic terms, the essence of these views is that, as in a hologram, every particle has full information about the "whole image," every cell of the brain (Pribram) has full information about the whole brain, and every particle in the universe (Bohm) is a manifestation of the "whole" universe. In Indian vedantic philosophy, the terms used are "Atman" (the individual self) and "Brahman" (the cosmic self): the microcosm is the macrocosm. Every cell of our body has a DNA which contains full information about the whole body. One can, therefore, in a sense, reconstruct the whole body from one cell: cloning.

Consciousness-related experiences

The third mode of perception is related to your state of *consciousness*. The ancient yogic and meditational processes enable you to experience different states of consciousness. There are several levels or states of consciousness, as described in detail on pages 109–111. Reality is state-specific – your perception and experience of reality depends on your level of consciousness, as described in chapter 9.

The Nature of Your Self

What, then, is the relevance of these various models of reality to you as a manager? In fact, your self is conditioned by your model of reality. As such, you can view your self in a variety of ways.

The Mechanistic View

On the basis of the Cartesian–Newtonian "materialistic, mechanistic, positivist, and reductionist world view" you would see yourself as a skin-encapsulated entity, consisting of skeletal, muscular, neurological, and other subsystems.

The Systemic View

On the basis of the quantum relativistic view of reality, you would see yourself as a "complex web of interrelationships, energy or wave patterns," or simply as some kind of "order" or "consciousness."

From this point of view every individual human being is essentially a part of a larger wave or a system, or energy pattern. In such a systemic pattern, you are perceived as a part of the entire reality or environment. Your skin is only a dividing line between the larger system outside the skin and the subsystem within the skin, as shown in Figure 10.3.

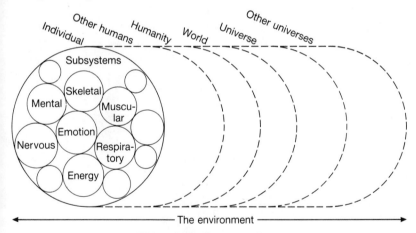

Figure 10.3 Quantum Reality.

Every human being is therefore perceived as a part of a "holarchy," ranging from the subatomic wavicles which combine into larger, "higher," and more complex systems to an almost unlimited, unknown environment. We are a part of and also *consist* of physical, chemical, biological, sociological, and ecological systems. A human being is an individual in five billion on a small planet in a little solar system in one of the galaxies.

The Evolutionary View

Now we look at the concept of the self in an evolutionary perspective. From birth onwards, an individual develops different levels of identity. At birth, an infant identifies with its biological functions. After several weeks, an awareness and experience of its *body* takes place and the infant begins to identify with the body. As you continue to grow, and as a variety of environmental inputs such as sounds and words begin to develop meanings in your mind, you begin to experience thoughts, and a stage comes when you identify with your thoughts, and *mind*. With education and further growth and interaction, you develop an identity as an *individual*, a distinct entity, a personal *ego*. At this stage, you identify with your ego personality.

The interesting point to note is the progressive, or cumulative, nature of these identity changes. At each higher level the previous

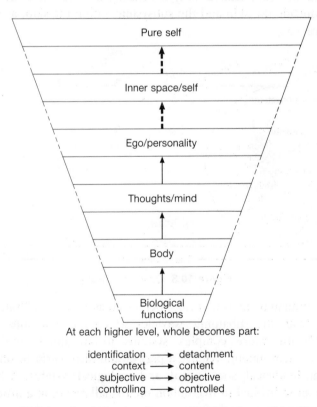

Figure 10.4 Levels of Identity: Progressive Detachment/Identification.

identity, or "whole," becomes a "part" of the next larger (or higher) level of identity, as shown in Figure 10.4.

With each shift in your level of identification, there is also a shift in the level of control. When you move from identification with your biological functions to the level of identification with your body, you begin to control your biological functions from the level of identity with your body. Likewise, when you progress or grow from the bodily identity to a mental one, you can control – from the mind – your body as well as your biological functions. Similarly, your ego level controls your mind or your thoughts, your body as well as your biological functions.

Moreover, at each higher level there is a shift from identification to detachment, from context to content. The subjective becomes the objective, and the controller becomes the controlled. The implication is that *you can control or manage that from which you are detached or "de-identified." Similarly, you are controlled or managed by that with which you are attached or identified.* This is significant, and must be understood, if you want to pursue a path of personal growth and development as an individual, and as a manager. The process of disidentification ultimately leads to the emergence of your true identity: like the peeling off of onion skins.

In fact, the next higher level, beyond the personal ego, is the inner or the deeper self (or level of "being"). If you are able to comprehend, reach, and experience this level of "being," then it becomes a strategic vantage point. From here you can control and influence ego identity or personality, and indeed change your personality or management style if you want to do so.

The crucial thing to note is that as long as you remain identified with the level of the ego, your life and work is run by it. If you want to alter your traits, your "type," or your attitudes and behavior while remaining at the "ego" level, you would find it almost impossible to do so.

The Psychological View

From a psychological perspective, there are at least four different perceptions of the self. In fact, it is the lack of congruence between them that causes stress (see Figure 10.5).

This viewpoint, "who we want others to think we are," is particularly stress-generating because, to a significant extent, it exerts pressure on your thinking, feeling, and behavior. Of course, this depends on the discrepancy between what we want others to think we are, who we think we are, and what we really are. One of the objectives of this book is to help maximize the overlap or minimize the discrepancies amongst all these perceptions or images of your self.

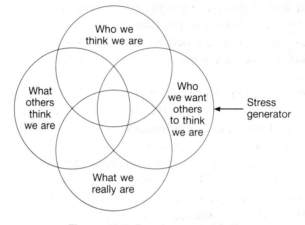

Figure 10.5 Four Images of Self.

The Functional View

At a practical level, you can also look at yourself as an operating organization, with its own functional areas; namely body, mind, and emotions. This viewpoint can be presented in the form of an organization chart (Figure 10.6) which shows your body, mind, and emotions as separate divisions, each one having subdivisions within it.

The most significant aspect of this organization chart is the positioning of your "self" as the managing entity. In this context your

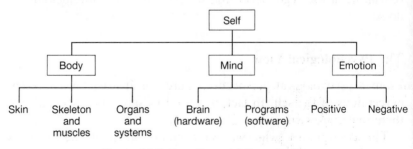

Figure 10.6 Your Personal Organization.

"self" strategically manages the three operational functions of body, mind, and emotion, through which the observing self operates, and attempts to create the kind of experiences you want from life. A more dynamic model, of the self as "managing executive," is presented in Figure 10.7.

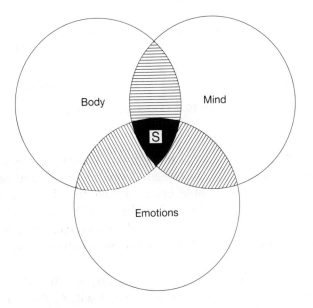

Figure 10.7 Self as the Managing Executive.

This deeper, reflective self is the strategic point from where you can manage yourself, your work, and your life. It establishes the context for the kind of experience you choose to have, and the goal congruence that you want to, or need to, bring about. Figure 10.8 shows how you can operate, within (yourself) and externally (your roles), remaining constantly in touch with or positioning yourself as the "managing self," and giving to yourself the experience you choose to have and the goal congruence that you want or should bring about.

This all becomes possible because it is at this deeper level of self that you can tap the potential, and the various faculties and competencies, that are required in the performance of your various roles. It is, in essence, the fact that you are detached from your operating self which gives you the kind of control and "managerial power" that you need in order to utilize your channels of operation more effectively.

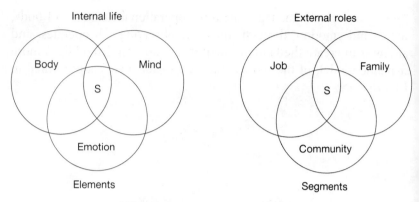

Figure 10.8 Dual Aspects of Self.

In fact, if you want to, you can control or change your perceptions, and thereby become less reactive and more self-reliant and proactive. You can make this possible either by altering the state of your consciousness (switching on or identifying with the observing self) whenever required, "centering" as explained on page 100, and/or by altering your intellectually based reasoning whenever it is dysfunctional.

We now turn from your self in society, which dealt with the possible identities and positioning of your self, to the notion of a return on investment (ROI) on your self, on your life.

11

Return on Investment (ROI) on Your Self

Experience a Difference

The objective of managing your self, as stated earlier, is to achieve success in your various roles, without negative stress and maximizing the satisfaction or ROI (return on investment) on your life. Basically, this involves stress management and self development.

If some of the concepts and processes discussed so far are pursued with diligence, over a period of time there would be a qualitative difference in your life. Instead of experiencing conflicts and tensions, you would remain centered and proactive, as illustrated by the following series of cartoons:

AT BREAKFAST

You would begin the day in peace, harmony, and joyful interaction with your family. Even while commuting from home to work or vice versa, whether standing in a queue or sitting on a train or bus, or driving your car, you could take the opportunity to do the centering exercise (see page 100). This would not only eliminate the external tensions, thereby preventing energy expenditure, but also serve to recharge your self through relaxation, re-establishing or consolidating your proactive posture:

IN ANY QUEUE

IN A TRAIN OR A BUS

IN A TRAFFIC JAM

However, even though you may have made all the necessary efforts to reach your destination, there are occasions when unexpected problems arise, distorting and delaying your plans. Symbolically, this could be illustrated by the following cartoon, conveying a situation in which your flight has been delayed:

AT THE AIRPORT

INFORMATION

WAITING FOR FLIGHT DEPARTURE

No matter how upset you feel, you cannot do anything about the delay, as the flight is delayed due to several external factors over which you have no control. However, after having ensured that you have made all the efforts that you can, no useful purpose is served by remaining tense or upset. (This is, in a sense, nonchangeable "gravity"!) Instead you could use the time you have available for meditation and re-energizing yourself!

There are many involuntary delay periods in life, such as waiting in a queue, at the traffic lights, or even for the lift. You have the choice as to whether to become tense with impatience, that is suffer negative stress, or to practice centering and recharge your self as shown below:

WAITING FOR THE LIFT

By practising centering and meditation on occasions which normally cause you stress, you can alter your experience from a negative one to a positive one, your posture from a reactive one to a proactive one, and your being from self-centeredness to a comfortable and confident centeredness in your deeper self: achieving high performance and success without stress and with satisfaction, as symbolized in the following cartoon:

AT ANY MEETING

How can such a state be sustained? For this we now turn to ways and means of sustaining peak performance.

Sustainable Peak Performance

Maximizing the return on investment on your life, the objective of "managing your self," implies achieving sustainable peak performance, leading others, and transforming organizations. In the light of the concepts and dimensions of the self described so far, I now want to review these three basic outcomes of managing your self.

We all experience stress to varying degrees. In fact, you require a certain amount of stress to stay alive and to remain active. If you do not experience a degree of stress you will be understimulated. Understimulation causes boredom, frustration, dissatisfaction, and fatigue, while overstimulation results in tension and a feeling of unrelenting pressure.

However, there is a middle zone where you are neither under- nor overstimulated. This is the peak level of "being" (see page 44). There is tremendous excitement without tension, a complete absorption in the task being carried out – performance happens! It is almost effortless and is described as a flow state, a peak experience. At this peak level of performance, you feel intense joy and satisfaction, even ecstasy. In this state you access and actualize your deeper potential.

In this state, there is no distraction from inner mental dialog: there is no noise from the ego. What you experience is inner music. You are merged – you identify completely – with what you are doing. You feel at one with the task in hand. What shows up is not yourself, but your performance: you become your performance. This may either be seen as an altered state of consciousness or as another way of describing peak performance.

So how do you gain access to and maintain such a level of performance? There are three processes involved, each of which has already been discussed earlier, but it would now be useful to recapitulate.

1 *Altered logic*   This is achieved by altering your frame of mind, or thinking style; cultivating a different kind of attitude toward whatever you are performing. This frame of mind, or attitude, has been discussed through the illustration of a long-distance race (pages 89–92). The logic of "detached" runner B is more likely to result in peak performance over a sustained period. "Attached" runner A may generate momentary peak performance (not peak experience), but he will not be able to sustain it, owing to premature exhaustion. Sustainable peak performance is possible when, through an appropriate attitude and logic, you detach yourself from your ego and from the results themselves, and identify yourself with peak performance and peak experience. In other words, you shift your psychic identification from result to efforts, from target to process. This should serve to release your attention, and energy, from the "fear of losing" (the result) to the "joy of doing" which, in turn, should lead you toward even bettering your best.

2 *Altered neurosensory programming (NSP)*   As I mentioned before (see page 104), your thoughts, feelings, and actions are largely influenced by your underlying drives and programs. A significant proportion of your thinking is visual and image-based, and you store an awful lot of negative images and programs in your mind. You will also have noted that when you think about your performance in some important future event you sometimes experience discomfort or "butterflies" in your stomach. This

results from negative images, or programs, which become self-fulfilling prophecies. Therefore, by initially identifying such negative programs, you can subsequently substitute them with positive ones, by envisioning and mentally simulating peak performances through deliberate exercises to heighten sensory perception. In effect, you use enhanced audiovisual and kinesthetic skills to create more effective and high-performance triggering internal programs.

3 *Altered consciousness, involving "becoming by being."* As already indicated (see page 91), you can do more and feel better by creating psychic detachment: you detach yourself from your ego by "centering" your "self," thereby moving away from self-centeredness and result orientation toward being centered in your self, leading to effort orientation through detached involvement. Such deeper "centering" is the key to your attaining sustainable peak performance.

Peak performance or excellence does not consist only in doing extraordinary things. It also implies doing ordinary things in an extraordinary way. It is not merely doing one thing 100 percent better. It also means doing 100 things even 1 percent better! It becomes a way of life.

12

Management by Detached Involvement

Becoming a Master Manager

One of the most interesting features of emerging organizational cultures and managerial styles is the changing managerial role model. No longer is it enough for a manager to have only analytic or problem-solving skills. These are being increasingly met by computers, and by expert and knowledge-based systems. What is of growing significance, in the new managerial role, is skill in leadership, particularly in these contemporary times of rapid and complex change.

In fact, if you reflect on the historical evolution of management, from the beginning of this century, you will find that managerial theory and roles, at any given time, have generally been based on the prevailing concepts of "man" (see Table 12.1).

Table 12.1 The evolution of management thinking

Date	Concept of man	Management approach
1900–1925	Rational–Economic man, social Darwinism	Carrot and stick approach, "scientific management"
1926–1950	Social man, "leaders are made, not born"	Human relations school, the Hawthorn experiment
1951–1975	Humanistic man, need hierarchy	Human resource management, Theories x and y, group dynamics, Maslow's need hierarchy
1976–1990	Holistic man, holarchy	Developmental management, Theory z, quality circles
1990–	Integrated man, "being" & "becoming"	Transformative, Synergistic approach, management

From Table 12.1 you can see that the contemporary concept of "man" is "enlarging" beyond the "ego level" of a human being. Consequently, the emerging approach in management is one of integration and transformation. This involves a synthesis between your self-centered, ego level needs and your self-less consciousness as a transcendent being. You then experience a kind of self-ness, operating from an integrated and "balanced" level of being. Such transformative and synergistic approaches alone can bring about, on a sustained basis, the kind of goal congruence – at a micro and macro level – that is now being increasingly expected from organizations, and therefore from managers.

In fact such "master managers" are expected to perform the multiple leadership roles of "focalizer," "facilitator," "synergizer," and "co-creator:"

- Focalizer, generating shared vision, mission, position, and attention
- Facilitator, bringing about commitment, action, harmony, and growth
- Synergizer, helping to achieve individual/organizational/societal role/goal congruence
- Co-creator, positioning oneself as co-learner and co-shaper of success – the first among equals, not the "hero"

In that leadership capacity they need to balance, and integrate, the economic and technological goals of business with the ecological and psychosocial aspirations of society, through a shared vision and committed action. In order to understand the complexities involved, and be able to achieve such goal and role congruence, you need, as a manager, to develop a higher level of *creativity*, a deeper level of *consciousness* of detached involvement, and the associated *knowledge*, *skills*, and *attitudes*.

Knowledge

As such a master manager, firstly you possess general insights into people, things, ideas, and events, as well as particular professional and managerial know-how. Secondly, you have greater insight into environmental forces and trends than is required for everyday business and management functions. Thirdly, you have in-depth insights into your own inner dynamics, covering the functioning of your body, mind, emotions, neurosensory system, and states of

consciousness. In other words, you know enough about your internal
dynamics and your organization's dynamics to be able to effect
harmony between the two.

Skills

The skills you have acquired, as a master manager, can be identified
and exercised at three levels: personal, group or team, and cultural.

1 *Personal*   At the *personal* level, you possess skills that enable you to
achieve inner balance and integration within the five dimensions of your
self – body, mind, emotion, neurosensory system, and consciousness.

2 *Team*   At the *team* level you have three types of skills:

(a) The skill of *motivating* others in a group, by linking their
interests and ideas to a common vision generated by the interaction
of these very interests and ideas, which serve to galvanize the
disparate group into a cohesive team.
(b) The skill of *communicating*: through a two-way process
developed through listening. It is only through such two-way
communication that you will enable every member of a team to
become clear about where they fit in the general scheme of things.
Similarly, through such mutual interaction, individual tasks and
team objectives are aligned – toward the commonly perceived
corporate goals and vision. This leads individuals to the kind of
commitment required of them in order to function as a team.
(c) The skill of "*facilitating*": within the framework of the team,
developing a structure as well as processes, which enable everyone
to perform at their peak level, within the context of the common
vision and mission.

3 *Cultural*   At the third, *cultural* level, you can develop alignment in
the organization, and attunement within the individual. These two
processes, when combined, serve to generate the necessary goal
congruences and to develop and maintain the vision and the mission
of both individual and organization.

Attitudes

Finally, as a master manager you have a particular set of attitudes. In
fact, you shift from traditional, power- and problem-driven attitudes

to vision-driven ones. These attitudes arise from your commitment to certain purposes and values. This implies a shift from a management style based on control and aggression to one centered upon caring and connection. Your thoughts, feelings, and actions are proactive and self-reliant as opposed to the conventionally reactive postures of many "innocent" or even professional managers.

Creativity

The fourth dimension in the master manager's leadership mix is that of creativity, which comprises the following elements:

(a) The capacity for *envisioning* and an understanding of *intuition*.
(b) The ability to have a much wider and deeper *perception* – the ability to see more than "what meets the eye."
(c) To see deeper significances and *connections*, which may not be obvious, and the ability to break old connections and make new ones.
(d) The skill to convert such connections into concrete *applications* relevant to the organization and its mission.

In other words, creativity implies a capacity for vision, intuition, perception, connection, and application.

Consciousness

The fifth dimension is that of consciousness, the capacity to shift your "gear" into different levels of consciousness appropriate to the tasks and the situations you are involved in. On the basis of your concept of reality and the self, you can develop an understanding as well as the capacity to access different states of consciousness, and lucidly tune into them whenever desired. This is possible when you are in touch with your deeper level of the self or consciousness which is detached from your ego self or from ego-related consciousness.

A master manager is usually neither "selfish" nor "selfless," remaining in touch with the deeper level of the self, that is, with his being-level. This could be described as "self-ness" – a kind of detached involvement. This removes the distraction of the ego-related "noise" and brings you in touch with your "inner music." Operating from such consciousness, you can access and achieve your deeper potential and perform with a "joy of doing" (not with a "fear of losing") so that you identify with current performance, in the context of the vision of the organization. This is the stuff of which sustainable peak performance is made. This is the most basic dimension of a leader, or "master manager," because it is this quality which inspires others. Finally, this is the level at which you experience alignment, attunement, and empowerment within the organization, and with its external environment.

Such mastery is therefore more a mental state than a personality trait. It can be learnt or cultivated.

From this perspective, it is clear that the "role" of the manager has shifted and has been enlarged, significantly, from that of the traditional problem-solver to that of focalizer, facilitator, synthesizer, and synergizer. Such synergy, at both a micro and macro level, is an essential precondition for organizational effectiveness, over the long term. Such "effectiveness" incorporates high-level performance and satisfaction of the individual and, at the societal level, rising standards of living and higher standards of life.

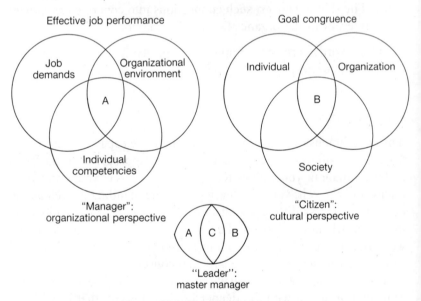

Figure 12.1 The Master Manager.

This implies that the master manager is one who is not only a good manager in a corporate context, but is also a good citizen in the social context. As a manager, in the organizational perspective, as shown in Figure 12.1, for effective performance he needs those competencies

"A" which synchronize his personal growth with his job demands and organizational enrichment. As a citizen, in the cultural perspective, to achieve goal congruence among the individual, the organization, and the society he needs qualities "B." As a master manager or leader, therefore, he needs the core of both "A" and "B," namely "C." This is the mix of knowledge, skills, attitudes, creativity, and consciousness that we have just discussed. These are attainable and sustainable with detached involvement which implies a larger, deeper, and richer vision.

On Being Vision Driven

I have presented the entire concept of "managing your self" and becoming a master manager within the context of development at three levels: societal, organizational, and individual. At the societal level the main forces that influence development are the ideologies prevailing in that society and its institutional framework. At the organizational level it is culture and structure that predetermines organizational development. Finally, at the individual level it is the totality of that person.

The approach I have adopted is basically a functional one. I have treated "self" as a "managing self." Through it you manage the various operating dimensions, or functional areas of your being, and through them your multiple roles in life. This enables you, in turn, to reach a higher level of consciousness. By operating at such a heightened level you should be able to enhance much of your hidden potential. As a result, not only can you grow and develop, to a much greater extent, as a human being, but you can also achieve the kind of success and the amount of satisfaction that you seek. Finally, you should create, in your immediate environment, a kind of "vibration around your self," which has a positive and powerful impact on those with whom you interact.

In essence, "managing your self" is about being *vision driven* rather than problem driven. In other words, managing your self is about re-visioning, implying renewal and a process of "rebirth." (Figure 12.2.)

At an ordinary level of consciousness, you would be conditioned to living and working in a "disease mode," or in a problem driven mode, because your basic approach would involve identifying problems, as success consists of solving problems. In other words, you would remain within the problem–solution cycle. Therefore development or

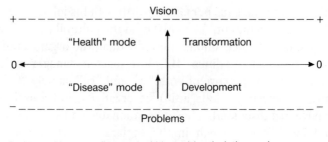

Problem-driven: confinement within problem/solution cycle,
                 propensity of problemizing

Vision-driven: problems seen as opportunities,
                enlarging context/making limitations irrelevant,
                making adversity work for you

Figure 12.2 Re-visioning (Renewal/Rebirth).

success would be marked by the absence of problems. In fact, with such a focus on problems, you would experience anxiety which generates negative stress; whereas if the focus is on "possibilities" with a clear vision, you will experience more positive energy as shown in Figure 12.3.

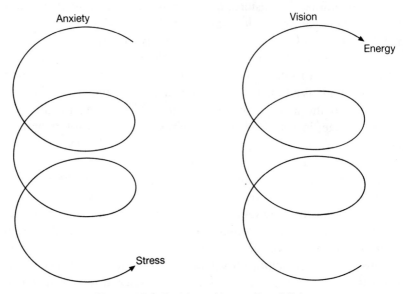

Figure 12.3 Problems Versus Possibilities.

As I have emphasized right from the start, the master manager's reference point is not absence of problems, nor absence of illness. It is rather the presence of wellness and the experience of an invigorating joy. Such joyful experience is possible only if you have a very clear vision before you, and thereby operate in the "health mode." It is in this mode that peak performance happens, concomitantly with peak experience.

To ensure such a level of peak performance, then, you need to have, first, a *vision* that is a very clear image of what your work and life is about. It is a kind of a dream: without a dream there cannot be any lasting excitement. This is becoming even more relevant and important in the context of accelerating change, complexity, uncertainty and conflict. It is through a clear vision that you will be able to experience a "quantum leap" (instead of just an incremental improvement) and acquire the necessary strengths: what Ilya Prigogire might call an "escape to a higher order".

Secondly (see Figure 12.4), to enable you to convert such a vision into reality, you have to verbalize it in a statement, a *mission* – a statement about your own life. Thirdly, you have to make a very clear stand or *position* on this mission. In other words, you have to commit yourself totally to the achievement of that mission, giving to it whatever it takes.

Once you have determined the vision, mission, and position you need, to align all your resources – human and otherwise – you provide the *locomotive* power to finally move the entire organization's energies,

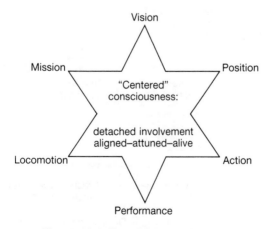

Figure 12.4 From Vision to Action.

single-mindedly and whole-heartedly, toward *action*. In the process you need to be able to sustain an ongoing creative tension. This ensures remaining "grounded" (but not "stuck in the mud") as well as "up in the sky" (but not in the clouds): becoming a "visionary pragmatist" or a "pragmatic visionary."

Peak performance and peak experience will then happen to you. You create the context in which what shows up is performance. You become transparent. You become the performance – you identify your consciousness with performance. You and your performance become the stuff of which creativity and excellence are made. You remain involved with performance and yet are detached from the results. This facilitates peak performance and its consequential upward spiral.

Organizational Transformation

The ultimate impact of self management with detached involvement is on the organization, leading to its progressive transformation. Having developed your self along the lines illustrated above, you should be able to synthesize the individual and organizational roles and goals, processes and results. If you want to transform anything or anyone, including any organization, you have to begin with your self. You need to reform and transform your self, through relevant education and meditation (outer space and inner space) as indicated in Figure 12.5.

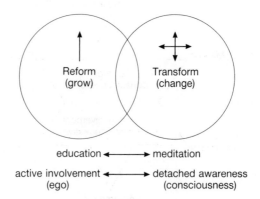

Figure 12.5 Self Development Through Detached Involvement (Re-visioning Renewal).

When working in or with a typical organization, you will find that the prevailing culture is usually a "reactive" culture which will need to be transformed into a "creative" one if peak performance is to result. To achieve this, you will have to go carefully and patiently through a series of steps. In fact, you need to start by changing the reactive culture into a "proactive" one. To enable this to happen you have, initially, to turn the entire organization into a "responsive" one. The process whereby you can facilitate this is by opening up discussions on the "purpose" and functioning of the organization: why it exists – its philosophy; what it is supposed to do – its ideology; how it is going to achieve it – its strategy. Through engendering such a learning process you can move the organization to a "responsive" stage.

Over a period of time there is more "listening," and a climate of deeper understanding of the individual, group, and organizational roles begins to pervade. Such goal congruence leads to more personal interaction, to an intensification of team spirit, and to a greater sense of "belonging" and "commitment." This sets the stage for a proactive culture, which forms the essential precondition for the development of a more interactive and "creative" culture, when the organization becomes "vision driven" – leading to organizational peak performance on a sustained basis, as shown in Figure 12.6.

In order to evolve from proactivity to creativity at the individual, group, and organization levels, you need the qualities and competencies of a master manager, which are the natural consequences of management by detached involvement.

This, then, is how you achieve an effective synthesis between your individual and organizational roles and goals, through a synergistic blend of personal and organizational transformation, as shown in Figure 12.7, which combines Figure 12.4 (personal vision) with Figure 12.6 (organization culture).

At this stage the individual, the groups, and the organization are fully aligned, attuned, and alive. Individual and organization have advanced beyond the Peter principle and the job, career, or life plateaux. This is what "managing your self" and detached involvement are all about. Figure 12.8 captures this idea by showing that the center of your being is a constant, strong, and stable pivot of consciousness, a base which liberates you into greater activity: "doing more" and at the same time feeling steady and secure and therefore "feeling better." This in turn facilitates and triggers even more activity and higher performance. The centered consciousness, or central pivot, is the perennial source of positive energy – much like the eye of a storm, which is a kind of silent, dynamic vacuum but is a source of all the energy in the storm. As stated earlier, this centeredness is like remaining in touch with the perennial light and energy of the sun above the clouds while coping with the storms below. Detachment might imply, in the ordinary sense, that you have to let something go. The interesting paradox about this is that, in fact, you get a better result in the activity you are pursuing by a certain degree of detachment. For example, when you are driving a car your performance with the steering wheel is better if you do not hold the steering wheel too tightly with both hands, but loosen your grip somewhat. When you are carrying heavy luggage in one hand, to keep balance you have to lean on the opposite side. It is this psychic distance or pull which is the difference that makes a difference.

Another metaphor that you might use to articulate this new and more effective "organizing principle" of detached involvement is that of a top: the top can spin faster if its spindle or pivot is steady. At the

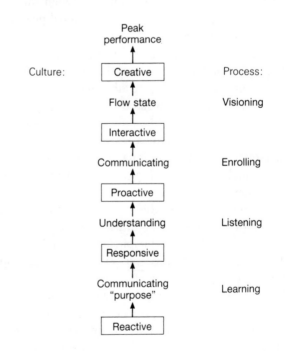

Figure 12.6 Making a Difference.

same time, the faster the top spins, the steadier the pivot becomes. This enables the top to spin even faster, and so on. Detached involvement thus helps you to become a "top" manager!

Therefore, to the extent that you manage your self with detached involvement, your life, career, or job becomes a continuous success story. Life is like a roller coaster: there will be ups and downs, and there will be difficult situations and complex choices, involving risks. But you should never escape risk-taking: in a sense, risk avoidance is

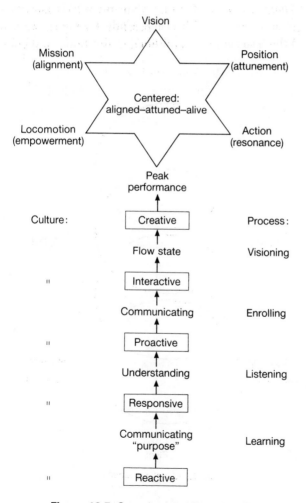

Figure 12.7 Organizational Transformation.

life avoidance. Detached involvement offers the courage to move with stillness in the world, instead of freezing into stillness in the face of accelerating change, uncertainty, and risk.

The Paradox of Happiness

The key to success is for you to align your expectations (of results) in a manner such that your basic experience, at any given point of time, is one of satisfaction. In other words, *satisfaction or happiness consists of "striving to get what you want, but at the same time experiencing the wanting of whatever you get."* Getting what you want is success: wanting what you get is happiness. This is apparently a paradox, but if you have understood the basic approach outlined in this book, and got in touch

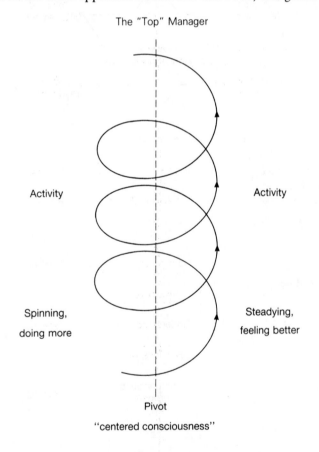

The "Top" Manager

Activity   Activity

Spinning,   Steadying,

doing more   feeling better

Pivot

"centered consciousness"

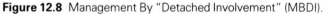

Figure 12.8 Management By "Detached Involvement" (MBDI).

with your deeper level of consciousness, you will have resolved the apparent contradiction.

You will be able to experience joy and satisfaction, then, while functioning in your daily activities, because you are drawing your basic satisfaction from the inner source of joy, and not from the results or rewards for which you strive in your external environment. The essence of excellence, therefore, is "management by detached involvement" (MBDI) – involved but not imprisoned, interested but not addicted. In essence, you are involved in the activities of your work and life, in your efforts to be successful, but you remain detached from the rewards themselves.

The Missing Link

The crucial dilemma for managers today is to resolve the continuing significant gap between the torrent of new management models they are exposed to in the contemporary literature and at seminars (and which they are expected to actualize), and their personal ability to do so: the gap between what managers want to do and are actually capable of doing, as well as between what they like to do and what they have to do. Management by detached involvement provides this missing link by raising the awareness and experience of, and identification with, a higher level of consciousness or self. This means becoming detached from the barriers and blocks of the ego self, which is responsible for the above-mentioned "gap". Moreover, this also results in greater empowerment and freedom, which are enhanced by the gradual change, maturation, and eventual disappearance of the self-limiting ego-consciousness or ego sense. Symbolically, this could be expressed as:

$$LET$$
$$G$$
$$O$$

With a constant awareness, psychic involvement, and identification with the deeper consciousness – the pure and perpetual self – and detachment from or "de-identification" with the changing, aging, and mortal ego self, you will be able to conquer even the fear of the ultimate loss – that of death. If you experience your ego death, you do not feel death when the body dies: your attitude becomes "the world dies, but I go on" rather than "I am dying and the world goes on." Death is seen as a transformational experience – not a point of termination. The essential elements of water do not die even when they change their form into ice or vapor. In this sense there is no death – only change in our cosmic address!

It is only when you operate from such a detached consciousness that you can bring about authentic organizational transformation. In the process you will be transforming organizational cultures from hierarchical structures into mutual support networks; from management styles based on control and aggression to those oriented toward "caring and connection." Moreover, in the final analysis, you will be transforming your role from that of either innocent or professional to that of master manager – a visionary pragmatist. Such a master manager knows how to do business in the new paradigm. This is the substance of our final chapter.

13

Doing Business in the New Paradigm

A Synthesis of Western Science and Eastern Wisdom

Managing Congruence

Values and "Isms"

Doing business in the new paradigm (or in the new, emerging view of the business world) starts with managing your self. A conceptual overview as a summary of the major elements of managing your self is provided in Figure 13.1. At the top, you can see the world systems or "isms" within which you create and manage your life. Several such societal "isms" or ideologies have been advocated and practised in different parts of the world during this century, with varying degrees of success (?) or failure. In fact, they represent different combinations of two basic parameters, values and ideologies, as shown in Figure 13.2.

The vertical "value-laden" axis covers the whole spectrum of values, ranging from the spiritual (emphasized in Eastern cultures), to the materialistic (dominant in Western thinking), from a self-denying to a self-centered approach. The horizontal "ideological" axis covers a different range of ideological stances. These extend from freedom of the individual on the one hand, to integration with society on the other, ranging from competition to collectivism, or from capitalism to communism. In fact, none of the value sets or "isms" have been able to achieve their stated objectives, namely societal growth and/or individual welfare, on an equitable or durable basis.

In this context of the existing paradigm of values and "isms," then, what is the average manager's approach to life? To cope with the rigors

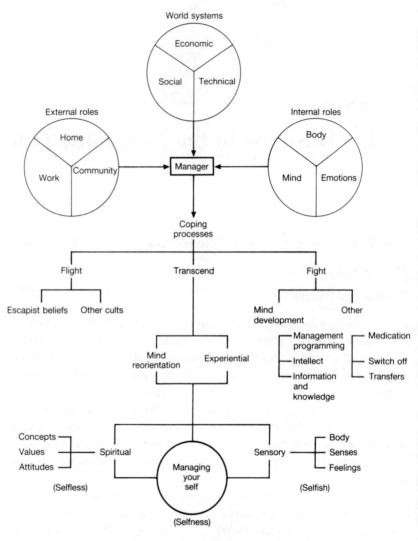

Figure 13.1 Self-in-the-world.

of accelerating change and uncertainty, complexity and conflict, managers generally adopt coping approaches which are either fight or flight. In other words, you either try to orchestrate external events (inevitably frustrating) or to escape from them (self-limiting). And for internal satisfaction, you either try to "acquire more knowledge" (with a hope of behaving differently) and/or take to medication, drink, or smoking, and so on. In other words, you basically try to gain some

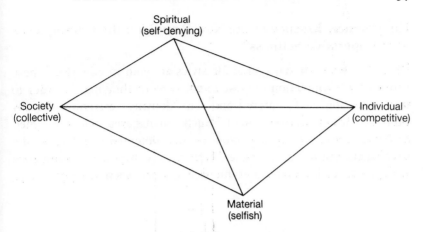

Figure 13.2 The Values–Ideology Axis.

comfort and peace from external sources – the result is continuing stress and frustration.

What is really required is a strengthening of your self, whereby you generate the capability within you to cope with accelerating change, and to overcome conflicts. The only "ism" that can work for everyone is "pragmatism." This implies no ideological or value bias, either Western or Eastern, and no compromises in between, but a cooperative synthesis of the two, at the top, as shown in Figure 13.3.

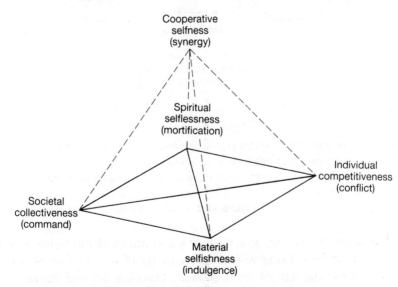

Figure 13.3 Self Managed Pragmatism.

Congruence: Essence of the New Paradigm; the Consequence of "Cooperative Selfness"

Behind or beneath managerial life styles are your mind styles. These involve a re-orientation of your mind, or your thinking, in order to transcend both self-centered and self-"denying" extremes, thereby evolving "detached involvement." Such a managerial style is designed to bring about an optimization of the potentials of you – the individual, your organization, and your society. In place of dominance or dependence is a congruent interdependence, seen in Figure 13.4.

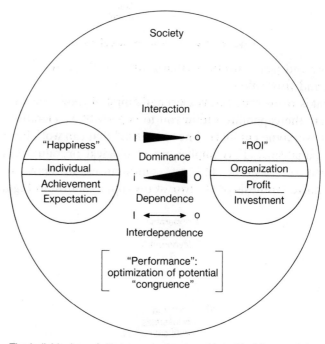

The individual needs the organization to achieve his full potential
The organization needs the individual to achieve its goals
Society needs organized individuals to attain a rising quality of life

Figure 13.4 Quality of Life.

This congruence can be achieved by a synthesis of the technology of how to make a living with the psychology of how to live; of the science with the art of management; reaching beyond business manager to business yogi!

The Paradigm Shift

"Raplexity"

This is the direction in which the world seems to be moving, almost imperceptibly but quite unmistakably. This is the paradigm shift which is being increasingly talked about now in mainstream business forums. The tabulation below will facilitate translating these basic trends into meaningful implications at the microlevel, for managers:

I
- Quantitative   Transience "raplexity"
- Qualitative   Revolutions:
  agricultural → industrial → technological
  information --→ consciousness

II
- World view   Mechanistic → holistic --→ holographic
- Concept of man   Economic → social → humanistic →
  holistic --→ transpersonal
- Values   Competitive --→ cooperative
- Thinking   Analytic → creative --→ intuitive
- Living   Survival --→ resonance

III
- Concept of wealth   Land → cattle → money →
  information --→ consciousness
- Role of business   Power-driven → purpose-driven --→
  planetary
- Organizational culture   Power → role → achievement --→ support
  purse/person --→ vision
- Management style   Control and aggression (threat/stress)
  Caring and connection (trust/energy)
- Role of manager   Problem-solving --→ leadership
  Fear of losing --→ joy of doing

The constant *change* that is going on around you is both *quantitative* and *qualitative*. The magnitude and pace of quantitative change is so great that it has been described as "raplexity," meaning a combination of rapidity and complexity. The nature of the qualitative change consists of layers of simultaneous revolutions, ranging from the agricultural to the informational.

The most commonly acknowledged contemporary change is the "information" revolution. However, there are already significant signs of a thrust toward a "consciousness" revolution. In fact, Willis Harmon describes today's paradigm shift as a movement from the first to a second "Copernican revolution." The first Copernican revolution created more accurate awareness and understanding of "outer space" and the positioning of the earth as a satellite in the Solar System. The second "Copernican" revolution is expected to generate greater insight and consciousness into your "inner space," thereby positioning your "self" and your life space in the context of an appropriate "reality."

The *world views* or the paradigms of "reality" are also changing from the "mechanistic" ones that have prevailed over the past few centuries, based on the Cartesian–Newtonian model, to a holistic and holographic world view based on the quantum relativistic model (see Figure 13.5). Ronnie Lessem has also referred to this in his book on *The Learning Organisation.*

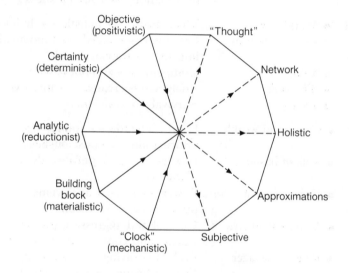

Figure 13.5 The Paradigm Shift: Changing World Views.

The mechanistic view has been based on the notion that "to understand the whole, you must understand the part." The holistic view maintains that "to understand the part, you must understand the whole." Finally, the holographic view suggests that "the part is the whole." The old paradigm's focus is on management of observed systems: the new paradigm could be viewed as management of observing systems.

It is interesting to note the convergence of this view, based on the "new" physics, with the ancient Indian vedantic wisdom. One of the Sanskrit verses in ancient Indian literature states:

This is the whole; that [part] is a whole. The whole [part] emerges from the whole. Even if the whole [part] is taken away from the whole, the whole still remains.

What is the relevance of all this to business? As mentioned on page 140, business policies and management thinking are based on particular assumptions about human nature. These assumptions have been changing during recent decades from a narrow *concept of man* as an economic entity to a broadened view – ranging from "social" to "humanistic" to "holistic." With the resultant growing interest in the whole person, a human being is now viewed not as independent of and separate from nature, but as an autonomous subsystem through which consciousness is manifested. Furthermore, consciousness is no longer a product of chance mutation amongst particles, but is considered as the ultimate reality. This is the transpersonal view of "man" who has both a self- (ego) centered existence as well as an ego-transcending, or transpersonal, self.

It is in the context of such a concept of man, that the *values* in business seem to be moving from adversarial competition toward more cooperative competition. This is manifested at the inter-organizational level, by the growth in mergers and strategic alliances and, within organizations, by the shift toward inter-functional teams and networking. As a corollary, the focus in managerial *thinking* is moving from the earlier emphasis on analytic problem-solving to a recent orientation toward creative abilities, and now toward intuitive insights. In fact, the whole attitude toward *life* is also changing from one of just surviving to one of meaningfully thriving and thereby "resonating" with all the other interrelated elements in life. This implies that "richness" or "*wealth*" is no longer evaluated in terms of traditional measures such as land, cattle, money, or even the contemporary notion of "information." Increasingly, "riches" are being assessed in terms of your capacity to experience higher levels of vision and consciousness.

This is being evidenced by a perceptible shift, as Charles Hampden-Turner has suggested, in attitudes toward the purpose and *role of business*. From earlier orientations toward profit and power, to a more recent focus on people, we are now seeing business leaders seeking greater alignment with global and ecological concerns. The internal corollary of such external "turning" is the growing interest in creating an *organizational culture* based on support systems, networks, and shared values, rather than on power, money, or personal ambition – changing outlooks through deeper insights.

There is therefore a rapidly growing shift in *management style* away from one based on control and aggression (which inevitably generates threats of "losing," leading to negative stress) toward one based on "caring and connection." Through the resulting team spirit and a "connective consciousness," you come to view your colleagues not as adversaries, in the management game of succession, but as co-creators of success. This in turn generates trust and therefore positive energy. Such are the qualities and competencies that are now being sought in *managers*. As more and more problem-solving skills are being taken over by computers and expert systems, it is leadership skills which are being increasingly required.

This is the essence of the new paradigm: the role of management is to create within the organization a climate, a culture, and a context in which corporate enrichment and individual fulfillment collaborate and resonate progressively in the development of a creative and integrative global community.

Managing Paradoxically: Transcending Conflicts

Doing business in the emerging paradigm, then, implies a basic shift in perceptions, purpose, and profiles of the organization and the managers from those in the old paradigm. Some of the contrasting characteristics of a business organization and individual managers, under the old and the new paradigms, are shown in Figure 13.6 and Table 13.1.

To initiate and achieve such a shift, individual managers need to cultivate almost contradictory or apparently paradoxical qualities, such as:

- Converging divergence
- Constructive discontent
- Flexible persistence
- Confident humility
- Relaxed attention
- "Mindless" perception

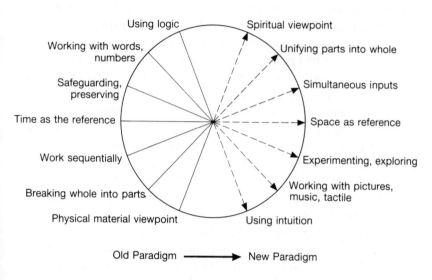

"Me in The World"   "The World in Me"

Old Paradigm ⟶ New Paradigm

Figure 13.6

Table 13.1   Contrasting management paradigms

Characteristic	Old paradigm	New paradigm
Strategy	Planned	Entrepreneurial
Structure	Hierarchy	Network
Systems	Rigid	Flexible
Staff	Title and rank	Being helpful
Style	Problem solving	Transformational
Skills	To complete	To build
Shared value	Better sameness	Meaningful difference
Focus	Institution	Individual
Source of strength	Stability	Change
Leadership	Dogmatic	Inspirational

How can one bring about such a radical qualitative shift in a corporate culture? How does one cultivate such apparently paradoxical qualities in a manager? This is where the relevance and significance of the concepts of the self – our real identity – becomes clearer. As already discussed, you have the potential to experience different levels of consciousness, and therefore self identities. With the practice of meditation and centering, you can remain "in touch" with your "deeper or observing self" – the self that is your "constant" secure pivot – and function through your ego, or operating or changing self. Isn't it interesting that we are described as "indivi-duals!" This also resolves the paradox of our conflicting urges: on the one hand we talk about, and want to, change; at the same time we want the security and comfort of all that we have and identify with, and at that level we do not want to change! Unless we can provide an experience of something better it will be almost impossible to enable anyone to let go of what he has!

As I have indicated (page 107), by providing yourself with an inner image of, say, a lemon (or whatever happens to be your favorite fruit), saliva happens to you, without your making any effort to create it! Similarly, by operating with such a dual or expanded consciousness, that is with detached involvement, you are able to cultivate even apparently contradictory qualities and become a master manager or a "business yogi." As such you gain, on the one hand, a synthesized experience of the nonchanging, undying, perennial, transpersonal self, a constant river of joyous energy, while interacting on the other hand through the ego self with constantly changing phenomena. This not only enables you to cope with change, complexity, and conflict, but also to master it. This transforms not only the quality of your mind but also your emotional profile and your physical chemistry. In effect you lead, or bring about change, through a synthesis (not a compromise) of several opposing or conflicting parameters, not only externally but also within yourself.

The common or traditional approach to conflict resolution has been one of compromise "in between" the opposing interests or viewpoints, which usually results in a win–lose or even a lose–lose settlement. Therefore such "settlements," whether intrapersonal, interpersonal, or intergroup, are most often neither satisfying nor durable. The synthesizing, synergistic, or "win–win" approach involves enlarging the "context" of any problem or conflict in any situation and enabling an understanding "above" or beyond the opposing or conflicting interests. This is illustrated in Figure 13.7, which expands a few examples of the basic conflicting attitudes listed below (source: psychosynthesis literature).

sympathy	_____	antipathy
excitement	_____	depression
blind optimism	_____	fearful pessimism

rebellion	————————	submission
self-deprication	————————	arrogance
intellectual doubt	————————	dogmatism
license	————————	depression
weakness	————————	violence

From Figure 13.7, you will find that the usual approach is to find a compromise, somewhere midway between opposing or conflicting elements of sympathy and antipathy, in the form of indifference. The genuine resolution, however, would be one of benevolent understanding of the broader context which causes sympathy or antipathy and thereby, through sincere empathy, find a lasting solution which satisfies both the extremes. This is possible if you are able to detach or distance yourself sufficiently and involve yourself adequately rather than have indifference. Similarly, you can, with such inner experience, bring about serenity, clearer vision of reality, and transcendence. The natural consequences of this are the paradoxical qualities we expect in a master manager – they happen to you!

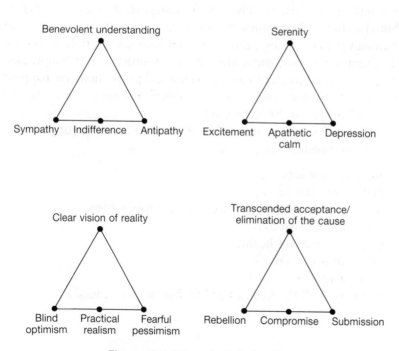

Figure 13.7 Triangular Relationships.

Synthesizing East and West

Such an "understanding" can also help us in taking a "clear stand" on some of the basic issues facing us today:

- Are you, as a manager, living for business or are you in the business of living?
- Are you interested in adding years to your life, or life to your years?
- Is your main interest in making yourself a living, or in making a life for yourself?

To be able to achieve a synthesis, beyond such either/or propositions, so as to secure a larger and inclusive "both," you have to combine the technology of "how to make a living" (Western management expertise) with the technology of "how to live" (Eastern philosophical traditions). You require a synthesis of the earning potential of corporations with the living potential of individuals. This also resolves the paradox of the old and new paradigms by enabling not only a symbiosis but a synergy between the two.

In other words, you should not only be "efficient" but also "effective," not only, as Warren Bennis says, do things right (a good manager), but also do the right things (a good leader). How do you ensure this? You may pursue money, power, and prestige – the symbols of success. As discussed earlier, these are pursued in order to feel happy. But, despite getting more of these we do not feel proportionately happier! We are, in a sense, going up the "ladder" but are we sure that the "ladder" is against the right wall?

The real issue is to remember that "success" or getting money, power and prestige can get us:

> food but not appetite
> clothes but not beauty
> a beautiful house but not necessarily a happy home
> books but not wisdom
> medicines but not health
> beds but not sleep
> even partners but not love
> and maybe all the luxuries of life, but not happiness!

Human Beings, not Human Havings!

Happiness can never come from "outside." This may be obvious – perhaps even a blinding glimpse of the obvious – but it is the obvious that is often overlooked! After all, you and I are described as "human beings," and not as "human havings," or even "human doings!" This is the essence of detached involvement. It is the missing link between success (getting what you want) and happiness (wanting what you get). Management by Detached Involvement enhances the drive to get what you want and, at the same time, enables you to thrive on what you get. Being to become!

Of course, living and managing by detached involvement requires courage. You have to change before you need to, and make your own space in time. Courage is the key, but fear seems to be the common reaction. Courage implies not absence of fear, but mastery over it. I therefore want to conclude by expressing an earnest wish that you enhance your courage to change what you can; enhance your serenity to accept what you cannot change; and, above all, always have the wisdom to know the difference. Perfection is sometimes described as the ability to live in harmony with the unchangeable imperfections in life!

Today is the first day of the rest of your life! Yesterday is a dream and tomorrow is a vision. Today well lived, as if it is the only one you have, makes every yesterday a dream of happiness and every tomorrow a vision of hope. What you *do* now determines what you will *be* in the next moment!

Index

images of self 129
imaging xv, 105, 106–8, 113, 163–4
impact, stress 43–9, 76–7
implementation *see* strategy
implicate order of reality xv, 126
implicit management consciousness *see*
consciousness
imposed limits 26
inadequacies 25–6
incompetence, level of 24–5
India *see* East
individual, evolution of 128
information revolution 119, 160
inner functions of management xi
inner music 115
innocent manager 29–30
inputs xiv, 104
insight 31
integrated performance of organization 8
intellectual drives 102; *see also* mind; thought
internal environment of organization 6–8
internal role conflict 36
intuitions 111
and creativity 143
investment in self *see* return on investment
involvement *see* detached involvement; new
paradigm
irrational (unrealistic) beliefs, converted to
PB 80–5
isms and managing congruence 155–7

Japan *see* East
job
performance 144
role 34–5, 37
joy *see* happiness; satisfaction
Jung, C. xi, 27

knowledge
and becoming master manager 141–2
not converted to performance 18
see also learning
Kundalini 109

lateral thinking xii, 63–4
leadership roles 141; *see also* master manager
learned manager 22–30
learning 18–22
additive and subtractive 18–20
believing is seeing 21–2
missing link 20–1
left brain 59–61, 105–6, 107
leisure *see* recreation
Lessem, R. ix–xvii, 160
levels
of existence 13–15

of living and managing 30–2
of self 13–16
life
cycle of 25
investment in *see* return on investment
living levels 30–1
positions 93–6; and personality types
27
quality of 158
limbic system 59–60, 110
list, master, for worries 98
literature of East 126, 161
locomotive power 147–8
logic, altering 80–97, 138
beliefs 80–7
comparisons 92–3
expectations 87–92
life positions 93–6
worries 96–8
logical thinking 63
lucid awareness 111, 115

mammalian brain 58–60, 110
management, principles of x, 7–10; *see also*
self
managerial, level of existence 13, 14
manifest order 126
manipura 109
martial arts xiii
Maslow, A. H. 27, 60, 110–11
master list for worries 98
master manager, becoming 140–45
attitudes 142–3
consciousness 143–4
creativity 143
knowledge 141–2
re-visioning 22–31
skills 142
mastery of self 23–32
dissonance, overcoming 23–4
level of living and managing 31–2
Peter Principle, beyond 24–5
re-visioning 29–31
seed principle 27–9
tapping human potential 25–6
mathematical thinking 63
MBDI *see* detached involvement, master
manager
mechanistic view of self 127
meditation xv, 112, 126, 136, 148
consciousness 112–15
mind
central nervous system 61–2
and consciousness 113
evolution of 128
intellectual drives 103
managing xii–xiii, 58–74